The Tuesday Morning Gang

Anthology

Compiled by
Charley Marvin

The Tuesday Morning Gang Anthology
by Charley Marvin

Characters

Acknowledgments

I would like to thank the following people who made this book possible.

First and foremost, the members of the Tuesday Morning Gang. Thanks for your patience, perseverance and ultimate belief in the fact that we might one day end up with a book about your fascinating lives.

Thanks to Tracey Stratton whose strong belief in this project got us through some tough spots. Without her enthusiasm, eternal optimism, organizational skills and wonderful photography, the result would not have been the same. Thanks also to Tom Keck for his professional photographic support. And thanks to Jane Schmauss for her able assistance and guidance in finishing the project.

I would also like to extend lifelong thanks to my head cheerleader, former legal secretary, and decades-old friend, not to mention her duties as editor of this book, Nancy von Neumann.

Finally, thanks to Brett Burner and his publishing company, Lamp Post Publishers, for compiling this book. Brett, you took what was intended as a spiral-bound softcover, and with your amazing professional vision, turned it into a real book. Thanks for your patience and unconditional support.

———————

With the unanimous agreement of all of the members of the Tuesday Morning Gang, in support of their mission to preserve surfing's rich history, all proceeds from the sale of this book will be donated to the California Surf Museum, located in Oceanside, California.

Charley Marvin
Encinitas, California
March 2018

Prologue

I would like to start with a quick introduction explaining the genesis of the collection of the Tuesday Morning Gang (TMG) biographies appearing in this anthology.

It began when I started gathering some historical stories about Leucadia for inclusion on the Leucadia 101 Main Street Association website.

As I got into that project, I recognized that there had been a number of celebrities who had lived on Neptune Avenue, Leucadia's beach street, which I renamed: "Neptune, the Avenue of the Stars."

After chronicling the history on the street of such resident luminaries as Charley Chaplin and the Eagles, I eventually recognized that, in addition to the movie and rock star celebrities, the piece required a Sports Division. I came up with the likes of Bobby Riggs and the Flying Tomato of Olympic and X Games fame, Shaun White.

Then an interesting thought struck me. Two of our own charter members of the TMG, Bobby Beathard and Woody Ekstrom, each definitely merited a place in this Leucadia sports pantheon.

So I did biographical pieces on both of them.

Then, although I'm very slow on the uptake, stuff usually eventually does penetrate the gnarly mass which constitutes my cerebral cortex. I had an AHA!! moment.

The thought struck me that within the membership of the TMG, we have an extraordinary number of fascinating individuals. Guys whose life stories were worth collecting and preserving for the individual members and their families.

And, VOILA, the project began.

I think this is an appropriate time in the "TMG Anthology" to reference the gang's roots.

There are two primary sources for the membership of the Tuesday Morning Gang. The first group is the Windansea gang. The second is the guys from LA's South Bay.

The Windansea crew consists of Michael Burner, Woody, his brother Carl, Tommy Carroll, and Clarkie.

The South Bay contingent includes just about everybody else; Howard Bugbee, Bobby Beathard, Jim Enright, Jim Thompson, Skip Stratton, Bill Taggart, and Tommy Dunne.

Then there are outliers like Tom Keck, who had to migrate all the way up from Coronado to join the La Jolla guys.

And then there is the ultimate outlier, your editor-in-chief/ group gofer/group historian; that would be me! I get the award for traveling the furthest to join this motley crew. All the way from a little town called Woodbridge, in Connecticut.

Elsewhere, in this anthology of biographies, I will deal with the history of all of these disparate characters getting together every Tuesday morning to make stuff up about what they have done in their lives.

Dear reader, because my reputation for hyperbole may have preceded me, you're probably assuming a large measure of embellishment on my part in claiming that the TMG is such a distinguished group.

Well, if that's your thinking, try these on for size:

What other group has amongst its members a gentleman who in his youth was one of the fastest runners in the world? What other group can claim that its members include an individual whom Sports Illustrated celebrated on its cover as "The Smartest Man in Football," soon to be enshrined in the NFL Hall of Fame?

If you dare, give me the names of San Diego based surfing icons who have had more historical impact on the sport than the brothers Ekstrom, Woody and Carl.

How about including in your membership a former fire chief, the man who set up the San Diego County helicopter firefighting service, who, in his spare time, has surfed three of the world's oceans?

And while you're at it, do you know who the original surfing pioneers were along the Central California Coast? Bet you didn't know that it was our own Bobby Beathard and Skip Stratton.

And what other group has among its membership a couple of the more famous paddlers from Southern California. Roy Bream who, in his prime, won multiple iconic Catalina to the Mainland paddling races, and Pat O'Connor, who was for eight years on LA County Taplan lifeguard competitive teams that never lost a surf or paddling contest.

The same Pat O'Connor who became a successful general contractor in the Newport Beach area before he went into the abalone processing business in Southern California and Tasmania, no less!

And the same Pat O'Connor who has been a private pilot. He is one of the four (count them – 4!) members of our gang that have been pilots; two commercial pilots and two private pilots.

———————

As another aviation example, how about our very own doctor, Chuck Lindsay, who made a dead stick landing in the black of night on the beach at Moonlight Beach. But that feat was small potatoes compared with the story of Chuck circumnavigating the entire coast of South America while piloting a small plane!

And if you're not impressed yet, how about Yuma Bill Taggart and Jim Thompson, who have been involved in more high seas' adventures than Captain Ahab and his crew.

If we still don't have your attention, I want to offer up a member, Tommy Carroll, who was part of the original core of Pan Am pilots, who traversed the Pacific Ocean in everything from piston-driven passenger aircraft, up to, and including, captaining 747s, all over the globe.

And the member that was a commercial pilot until a medical condition led to him becoming one of Aspen's ace ski instructors, not to mention engaging in his house-building skills in that area for some 30 years.

And finally, I have to ask you, what other distinguished group boasts among its members one of the original and best surf photographers ever, Tom Keck. The same Tom Keck who supplied Don Hansen with the shack in Hawaii where Hansen began his storied surfing industry career. Also, the same Tom

Keck who did his damndest to torpedo the nascent career of the transcendent surf and catamaran manufacturing behemoth, Hobie Alter.

And I haven't even mentioned our Emeritus members, Jim Enright and Richard Clark, both of whom have sadly passed on. Richard built one of the premier protective security device companies on the West Coast, when he wasn't surfing his beloved Windansea, directly in front of his beautiful beach home. In addition, Jim Enright, who was an extraordinary astrophysicist, bicyclist, surfer and bodysurfer (multiple world championships), and all-round great guy.

Well, are you finally starting to get the drift here . . . ?

In summary, I started this biographical anthology project because it suddenly dawned on me that I was surrounded by some of the most interesting characters one could ever hope to have the privilege of calling friends.

But what is the essence of this group? What is the common denominator/societal glue that got these gentlemen together in the first place and has kept them together for such a long period of time?

The answer is that the basic ethos of the group all derives from the ocean and ocean-related activities. Our Southern California ocean has provided the liquid adhesive (with a salty taste) that brought us together and keeps us together.

This group of men constitutes the gathering of some of the consummate Old-School Southern California Watermen.

Looking back into their personal lives, you will discover that, as a group, these individuals were there at the very inception of California surfing. They surfed with, and counted as friends, the original pioneers and icons of the surfing industry: Dale Velzy, Dewey Weber, Butch Van Artsdalen, Bob Simmons, Don Hansen, Leroy Grannis, Hobie Alter, Dempsey Holder, Miki Dora, Phil Edwards, Pat Curren, Bing Copeland, and more.

So sit back and enjoy this biographical journey from the beginning of the Great Depression through today's sadly chaotic world.

But before I run the risk of exhausting my limited vocabulary of superlatives, we need to address some administrative matters. These need to be dealt with prior to my introduction to you of the individuals that make up this fascinating group of gentlemen.

I'm offering the following in an effort to try to provide you with a taste of the elevated general tone mandated by our by-laws for the conduct of our weekly meetings.

At the risk of confirming for the reader your growing inclination to politely suggest that I find a new hobby other than writing, I humbly offer the following Memorandum that I submitted to the gang one Tuesday morning for its consideration at our meeting.

Memo

I submit that our group has been derelict for too long in failing to come up with an appropriate moniker for our Tuesday morning meetings.

Lacking such, we are presently at a severe competitive disadvantage in the exploding field involving the formation and operation of nonprofit, non-productive, coffee klatch group associations.

Although I fully recognize that by taking this initiative I am violating all manner of our group's unwritten rules and regulations, as determined by Skip, in his sole and absolutely random discretion. However, driven by the group's desire to aspire to our rightful place in the coffee klatch firmament, I am willing to risk a severe reprimand and/or banishment at the hands of our Fearless Leader.

Having covered all the "Whereases" and dispensing with all of the other totally useless preliminary legal jargon, I would like to submit the following list of potential titles for our group which should offer a new and fresh marketing appeal to our adoring public.

The suggested names which I am submitting for your esteemed consideration are:

- The Tuesday Morning Bored (not a misspelling!)

- The Seaside Geezers Club

- The Tuesday Morning Prevaricators and Marching Band

- The South Bay Yacht Club (Southern division)

- In deference to Woody, Carl and the other La Jolla refugees, the name: The Windansea Surf and Yacht Club (Northern division)

- The Seaside Market Breakfast Club

- In deference to most of our group's wayward and mispent youth and in special recognition of the illustrious life of one of our senior members, Howard, the name: The Poop Deck Alumni Association and Chowder Club (Founders Division) – So far, this one is my personal favorite!

- The (Way) Over the Hill Gang

- The Seaside Market Surf Team (in their dreams!)

These are just some quick suggestions. I would like to petition our Esteemed Leader (well at least some of the time) to take up the matter at today's meeting. Consider it a motion made. Do I hear a second?

Charley

The Tuesday Morning Gang

Anthology

- one -

Skip Stratton

We now have an opportunity to take a look at the life and times of the Fearless Leader of the Tuesday Morning Gang (TMG), Skip Stratton.

It's fitting that we start this biographical anthology talking about Skip. Somehow, someway, Skip managed to originally form, and then keep together, this disparate band of renegades for at least 20 years now.

Skip, I'm here to tell you, herding cats might have been a much easier task!

―――――

Skip's memory is not what it used to be, so I have collected some stories about Skip's life, with the help of his wonderful wife, Tracey, and his younger brother, Jim Stratton. I have also incorporated a marvelous piece written about Skip by his surfing buddy, Marty Coniglio.

―――――

It's probably Skip's fault. Depending on who you talk to, the TMG was originally formed down here at the Cardiff Seaside

Market (Skip's version supported by Roy Bream), or in the South Bay (Howard Bugbee's version). Either way, Skip was right in the middle of forming the TMG, so the group's conduct is most likely his responsibility forever.

Skip is a product of Hermosa Beach, the Northern Division of our gang.

He was born in the Torrance Memorial Hospital in 1940. Skip had two sisters and two brothers, including his younger brother Jim, who has contributed to this narrative.

It was his grandfather who named him Skip. The same grandfather who lived on the East Coast and, according to Skip, was one hell of a semi-pro baseball player back in the day.

Having been brought up on the East Coast myself and having played in some of those semi-pro leagues, I can tell you that the brand of baseball played in those leagues was fairly high. Skip indicated that he has found old newspaper articles of that era talking about his grandfather's many baseball accomplishments.

While Skip was still a baby, the family moved from 18th Street in Hermosa Beach, to Sierra Madre for a year. Next his family spent about a half dozen years in Orinda. Then, in 1948, they moved back to where it all started, Hermosa Beach, to a home on Monterey Street.

According to his brother, Jim, because the whole South Bay was connected, Hermosa Beach, although it was a very small town back then, was the center of most of that area's beach and water activities.

After they got back to Hermosa Beach in the late 1940s,

when Skip was still a kid, he loved to go to Longfellow Street for body surfing. Then there was 22nd Street to greet all of the girls coming down from Bakersfield. On the other hand, before they were surfing gremmies, he and his buddies went to 2nd Street at Bergstrom to rent surf mats.

He also loved to watch the Taplan lifeguard races conducted at Hermosa Beach.

———

But surprisingly, given the fact that we are so used to our gregarious Commander-in-Chief, Skip, Tracey claims that as a nine-year-old kid, he was quite a loner.

She claims he still is.

I might buy into that assessment that he's a quiet and reserved guy so long as the conversation with Skip stays away from surfing, football, grandkids' athletic achievements, his siblings, his wonderful wife Tracey, fishing, the former family place on Mammoth Mountain, (formerly) the Chargers, surfing buddies as a youth, the youthful adventures of Bobby Beathard and Skippy Stratton, and etc. etc. etc.!

———

But this morning Tracey offered me a marvelous historical visual in support of her contention that her life companion, Skip, was in fact a loner as a kid.

The story that she offered was this.

On occasion, when Skip was still only about nine years old, he would convince his father to let him ride his bicycle from Hermosa Beach up to the Manhattan Beach pier, to go fishing.

Now before any of you races to dial 911 to contact, albeit on a retroactive basis, LA County Child Protective Services, I need to remind you of something important.

Those were in fact the proverbial "Good Old Days." Nobody ever locked their doors and, unlike now, there was no requirement that parents constantly serve on helicopter patrol ensuring the absolute safety and security of their kids during every second of their young lives.

Back in the late 40s, we older folks can remember riding our bikes everywhere. When we took off every day, our parents gave us one admonition, and only one. "Make sure you make it home for dinner and before it gets dark!" That was it.

Wouldn't it be nice . . . ?

In any event, once young Skip got up to the Manhattan Beach pier and began fishing, looking down into the outside surf line up on any given day, he was likely to be watching Dale Velzy, Greg Noll, and Dewey Weber performing amazing feats on their surfboards.

This was well before anybody recognized that these guys were famous.

And our Skip would sit there and dream of the day when he could fly along the face of a monster wave, just like Dewey Weber.

I've seen a couple of Skip's surfing pictures that indicated he darn near got there!

Tracey shared that Skip was so excited when he got his first Velzy surfboard that he convinced an older gentleman in the Hermosa community, who was heavily into surfing, to take Skip all the way down to San Onofre to surf with him.

When it came to schooling, Skip was a Hermosa Beach kid all the way. He went to North School Elementary, Pier Avenue Middle School, and eventually to Mira Costa High School, in 1953.

At Mira Costa, he was seriously into sports. He played football, basketball, and ran track. As a track athlete, he competed in the high and low hurdles, and also ran the 440.

Obviously Skip was quite an athlete. However, at all of our gang's advanced stage in years, I feel compelled to acknowledge that I am having a little difficulty trying to get my head around a visual of Skip doing the high hurdles.

Of course by the same token, because of the full replacement of my right shoulder and my existing torn right shoulder rotator cuff, I'm also having difficulty conjuring up how I used to be able to throw football almost 70 yards in the air. Now, I can throw about 20 yards with my left arm and about 10 yards with my right!

Skip graduated from Mira Costa High School in 1957, when he was only 17 years old.

He was such a terrific athlete at the high school that he got a football scholarship from Cal Poly San Luis Obispo.

While in college, he was a punter, wide receiver, and also played defensive back.

It was also while he was still in college, in 1960, that Skip had to suffer through the type of tragedy that kids in college should never have to be exposed to.

The Cal Poly football team was flying to a Midwestern college game. Heartbreakingly, the team plane crashed in Bowling Green, Ohio, and 18 members of the football team were killed.

Fortunately, still strapped to his airplane seat, Skip's buddy Dick McBride was thrown out of the fuselage of the destroyed aircraft and launched out into the runway.

Although he was severely injured, Dick at least lived. So did another of Skip's friends, Ted Tollner. *[Query whether this is the same, or the father of, Ted Tollner who recently successfully tutored CJ Beathard, Bobby's grandson, to become a third-round draft choice of the 49ers?]*

According to Tracey, in the irony of ironies, after two near-death experiences within a very short period of time, Dick ultimately was killed in a car crash where the investigators believe he fell asleep and smashed into a tree.

An obvious question may have come to mind as you have been reading this enormously sad tale about the football team plane crash: "Why wasn't Skip on that plane with the rest of the football players?"

Because (miraculously) he had suffered a concussion in the football game on the previous weekend.

Due to the concussion, the team doctors and trainers ruled out his competing in the next game. The college had a new rule that you couldn't travel with the team if you suffered a concussion in the previous game. Therefore, Skip was left at the college while the football team traveled east on their tragic flight.

When you talk to Skip about this subject, he gets real quiet.

Last time he and I talked about it, he muttered: "Why me? Why didn't I die on that plane?"

The only answer I could come up with was that God had other plans for Skip.

And in fact God did!

Skip was one hell of a football player in college! He was so good that the Montréal Alouettes of the Canadian Football League advised him that they wanted to draft him out of college as a punter.

Skip politely declined the offer.

Employing irrefutable Strattonian logic, Skip reasoned: "Why would I want to go up to Montréal, Canada, to freeze my tail off playing professional football, when I couldn't even speak French?!"

[The following is a narrative of my concoction heavily relying on considerable information provided to me by Skip's younger brother, Jim. Thanks for the help, Jim!]

Except for the fact that, in Jim's words, their mom and dad made Skip take his younger brother along just about everywhere Skip went during the summer months, Skip's was an idyllic beach life.

Fishing off of the Manhattan Beach pier, and sleeping on the beach at night with his older friends, like Henry Ford, Mike Rogers, and Doc Tuthill. Skip out in the ocean all summer with his surfing buddies, Henry Ford, Freddie Pfahler, Jim Bailey, Ray Beatty, and Jim Piper, just to name a few.

In the wintertime, Skip and his friends would usually surfed the Hermosa pier because they had lockers there for their surfboards. Not only that, but they had a place to warm up when they got out of the water in a heated room that the lifeguards maintained.

In the summer, the surf gang migrated to 22nd Street, where, Jim relates, it was much less crowded. They stayed away from the Hermosa pier because in the summers the flatlanders came out to the beach and mostly hung out around the Biltmore Hotel and the pier. The reason was that's where all the food stands and bath houses were located.

Jim indicated that his big brother, Skip, gave him his first surfboard. In Jim's words, it was a Velzy model that was in pretty bad shape. Before he handed it over, Skip stripped the glass off and was going to reshape it.

Fortunately for Jim, fate intervened in the form of Greg Noll. Greg volunteered his services on the basis that he could do a much better shaping job than Skip.

Since Noll's shaping job on Jim's board, there has been a bit of a historical controversy about whether or not Jim's board was the first surfboard ever shaped by that subsequently very famous surfer, Greg Noll.

In any event, once Greg finished shaping Jim's board, Skip had it glassed for his little brother.

According to Jim, it got pretty cold surfing during the winter months at the Hermosa pier, Redondo breakwater, and the Palos Verdes Cove.

One day, in an effort to battle the bone chilling oceanic winter waters, Skip showed up at home proudly sporting a rubber shirt. Jim stated that the rubber shirt should not be confused with a wetsuit.

Skip did acknowledge to me that the rubber shirt added very little in the warmth department, but did provide additional buoyancy.

It was literally a rubber shirt that Jim thinks Skip bought at the Dive 'n Surf shop. It was so tight around the neck, arms, and waist that Skip would have to rub powder all over Jim Bailey in order to get the rubber shirt in place on his buddy's body. The same Jim Bailey who always wore a rubber shower cap out in the ocean, as he continuously proclaimed the theory that your body heat escapes out of the top of your head as long as it remains uncovered.

As Jim recalls, in 1957 Skip went away to college at Cal Poly, San Luis Obispo.

The next year Jim and a buddy decided to take a run up to the college. Since this was prior to the day of easy cell phone communication, they showed up unannounced at Skip's dorm room.

When they initially arrived, they were told that Skip and his buddies, Bobby Beathard and Tom Coulter, were out surfing.

Later Skip and Bobby took Jim and his friend around to the local surf spots at Pismo Pier and Shell Beach.

Jim swears that those three guys were the pioneers of surfing in this Central Coastal California surfing area.

For proof, he points to the fact that everywhere the three went surfing with Jim and his friend, they always were the only

THE TUESDAY MORNING GANG ANTHOLOGY

surfers out on the water. Not only that, but usually they had a very appreciative audience back on the beach, watching them surf, because surfing was such a novelty for the area.

[Thanks for the input Jim!]

––––––––––

This morning at our meeting, Tracey and Skip related that Bobby and Skip and their surf buddies, Tom Coulter, Bill Clemo, and Dick McBride, may have been the surf pioneers in other Central California Coastal areas like Avila Beach, Jalama Beach, and Santa Cruz.

These guys were willing to do anything to reach a good surfing spot.

For example, you have to travel 13 miles of a rutted dirt road from Lompoc to reach Jalama Beach. No wonder no one else had surfed it before they got there!

One thing that Skip kept emphasizing this morning. This was all in the pre-wetsuit days and the bloody coastal waters up in that region are colder than a witch's . . . *[kneecap].*

Their only remedy, to keep from losing portions of their extremities to liquid frostbite, was to race back up the sand and maintain huge bonfires on the beach in order to ward off the advanced stages of hypothermia!

––––––––––

Speaking of Skip's old buddy Dick McBride, this morning at our meeting Tracey and Skip shared two horrendous stories about Mr. McBride.

The first one had to do with the tragic airplane crash of the Cal Poly college football team plane which was described above.

The second one occurred around Rincon Beach. Shortly after the plane crash, Dick and some friends were traveling back to Cal Poly. Dick needed to use the bathroom but there were no facilities available. They stopped at Rincon so that Dick could "use the facilities." At the time Dick was still badly injured from the plane crash.

Sadly, the potty stop didn't work out too well for him. He fell some distance down onto the riprap.

I'm not sure where they were, but Skip and a couple of his friends heard about it and raced to the location of the accident. They were able to patch Dick up sufficiently to get him to a hospital. He had suffered severe injuries, including a ruptured spleen.

When I asked Tracey to help collect stories about Skip's fascinating life, she contacted his brother Jim, and his lifetime friend, Marty Coniglio.

Previously you read Jim's input into the project. Below we have set forth Marty's moving piece about his lifelong friendship with our Skip:

> "Hermosa Beach in the 1950s was a hotbed of skilled watermen. Men having returned from fighting World War II and Korea were home raising their families. As a bunch of young kids, we had no shortage of heroes to look up to. We would watch the recently returned vets ride waves on huge, heavy wooden boards, with ease and expertise. There was nothing more we wanted to do than learn to surf like those men. Unfortunately,

those boards were too heavy for us skinny 13 year olds. We were told that we would have to wait until we grew a little more and put some meat on our bones. We waited and practiced our wave reading and paddling skills on our surf mats. The older guys were shaping and glassing their board in their garages. Some boards turned out good; some not so good.

There was one hometown resident who changed all of that for good. His name was Dale Velzy. Velzy started shaping balsa wood boards under the Manhattan Beach pier. He had a cadre of young surfers who watched every move he made, and ultimately became world class themselves. Greg Noll, Bing Copeland, Rick Stoner, and Dewey Weber all eventually became known in the surfing world as great surfers and shapers.

It was common for surfers from Malibu to La Jolla to surf places like the Redondo Breakwater, 22nd Street, and Manhattan pier, because our South Bay Surfers would demonstrate their world class surfing abilities at their breaks. This was a period before surf movies and magazines, so the surfers' reputations remained inside the small California surf community.

All of us South Bay surfers were familiar with Miki Dora and Kemp Aaberg from Malibu, the Haley brothers from Huntington Beach, Pat Curren and the Ekstrom brothers from Windansea La Jolla and, of course, Phil Edwards from Dana Point; all world class.

We were associated with the 22nd Street crew known as the "Double Deuce Danglers." There was a pecking order based on skills developed to the point of any given surf session. For example, if Dewey Weber was in the water, chances were you wouldn't get as many waves that day. There were so many talented surfers riding 22nd Street that it was difficult to catch any waves. Henry Ford, Freddy Pfahler, D.O. O'Conner, just to mention a few. All mentored in one way or another by Dale Velzy. Velzy wanted all the top surfers to ride his boards so when they surfed Malibu or Windansea, they were riding Velzy boards . . . good for business.

When I was ready to transition from surf mats to a surf board, finding a board was problematic. $35 could get you a dinged up balsa board that may or may not be water logged from poorly patched dings. It was a "beggars can't be choosers" period in the climb to be able to catch and ride a wave. Summer nights were often spent sleeping on the beach with my pals Skip Stratton, his brother Jim, and 9 or 10 of our surf buddies. Up at the crack of dawn, paddle out and attempt to do a head dip or kick out the way Dewey did it.

The era that I call "Before they Became Famous" was leading up to the time when Hollywood found out about the California surf scene. The book and movie "Gidget" changed it all. Suddenly everyone wanted a surf board and woody, and the rest is history. Greg Noll, Dewey Weber, Miki Dora, Phil Edwards, Mickey

Munoz and so many surf pioneers elevated surfing from an activity that our "Hermosa" parents were sure was a path to poverty and ruin. Only a few shapers made a good living shaping boards. Surf movies and magazines, contests and surf wear have become a huge market, making millions for people, many of whom haven't even set foot in the ocean.

Us old Double Deuce Danglers got to taste the surfing life style in its purest form. Surf road trips to uncrowded breaks with friends who have lasted to this day."

———————

Thanks Marty for those wonderful memories.

Reading Marty's narrative reinforced the perception that Skip, along with many of our other members, were there at the very earliest beginnings of the surfing culture in Southern California, throughout this country, and eventually the world.

Sitting among this small band of men, still meeting in their later years, it never ceases to amaze me that this handful of guys witnessed and participated in the very inception of this world-wide cultural phenomena.

And you know what's even more amazing to me? Until we started collecting the biographies of the Tuesday Morning Gang, I didn't have a clue about all this surfing history.

Sure I knew that the ocean, and particularly surfing, was a common denominator among the gang. And, yes, I had heard plenty of surfing stories on Tuesday mornings.

However, it was only after I started collecting these biographies that I realized that our gang grew up amidst, or were among the members of, the tall timber iconic figures in surfing history.

And why did that come as such a surprise to me?

The answer is simple. There is another common denominator among this stellar group of men. The total lack of braggadocio.

This group of guys is extremely adept in the fields of self-deprecation and self-effacing humor. However, when it comes to bragging, not so much . . . .

So Skip, even though it has been a monumental task for you to keep this fascinating and disparate group together for so long, I think the results have been well worth the effort!

On behalf of the gang, Thank You!!

- two -

Bobby Beathard

Another long-time Leucadian, Bobby Beathard, is the former General Manager of two NFL teams. He was in the NFL in varying capacities for 38 years. During that time, teams he was involved with competed in seven Super Bowls, winning four of them.

Bobby was the reason that I became a member of the Cardiff Seaside Market Tuesday Morning Gang (CSMTMG), or Tuesday Morning Gang, to kind of shorten the moniker.

In other words, some 12 years later, it's all Bobby's fault that every Tuesday I'm still hanging around the Cardiff Seaside Market with this bunch of old duffers!

On a Tuesday morning in January 2005, around the time when I retired from my law practice in Cardiff, I was headed into the Cardiff Seaside Market to buy some groceries.

As I walked across the courtyard, I noted a bunch of gray haired guys, lounging around some tables. Much to my amazement, right there in their midst, was our hero, Bobby Beathard, who has always looked much younger than he actually was.

I walked over and said hi to Bobby. He introduced me to his friends. I asked him what the purpose of the meeting was. He told me with a straight face, that they were there attending a "board meeting." Being the smart ass that I am, my response was to ask whether it was a "board" meeting, or a "bored" meeting of a bunch of old guys.

I guess maybe I should've never asked the question because, before I knew it, "I are one"!

I took the first cut at Bobby's story based on his international Internet fame and my personal experiences with him as his friend and attorney.

I am in the process of sending it off to Christine and Bobby to see if we can add some actual facts to Bobby's life history.

Bobby was brought up in El Segundo, California, and until the last few years, when he moved back to Franklin, Tennessee, to be close to his children and his 14 grandchildren, was the consummate Southern California Waterman.

Today, he also is able to spend more time with his son, Casey Beathard, who is one of country music's top songwriters.

Bobby has a grandson who is currently seeking a spot in the Canadian Football League.

Another grandson, CJ Beathard, was the starting quarterback for the University of Iowa over the last two years. Two years ago CJ led his team to the Big Ten championship and then on to compete in the Rose Bowl. Football analysts are predicting that he will definitely be playing in the NFL next year.

Christine Beathard has just informed me that CJ has been working out with the son of the former coach, Ted Tollner, here in Southern California. However, CJ is planning on traveling back to Franklin to be with his family on NFL Draft Day.

[Newsflash: CJ was just selected by the San Francisco 49ers in the third round of the 2017 NFL draft!!]

––––––––

It was Bobby's love of the beach that brought him to Leucadia and a condominium home on Neptune Avenue.

He, and his younger brother Pete, who was the quarterback for one of the better-known USC football teams, and later went on to compete in the NFL as a quarterback for the Kansas City Chiefs and Houston Oilers, built the two condominium homes just north of Beacons Beach.

At the time, Bobby was the General Manager of the San Diego Chargers. In his free time, on most days he could be found hanging out with his fellow surfers at Beacons Beach.

He later sold this condominium unit and bought a beach-front home on the northern end of Neptune.

––––––––

Bobby's history was all about football. He attended Cal Poly and was the starting quarterback for their football team in over 30 games. His record as quarterback was 25 wins and 5 losses. Not too bad for a school that hasn't been generally recognized as a California football powerhouse. As a result, Bobby was inducted into the Cal Poly Hall of Fame in 1988.

While we're talking about Bobby's induction into Halls of Fame, a few months ago, Bobby was inducted into the NFL Washington Redskins' Hall of Fame.

At the time of the induction into the Redskins Hall, the

President of the Redskins talked about a commonly-known fact around the NFL. That Bobby should definitely have been placed in the NFL Hall of Fame by now. More on that below.

When Bobby graduated from Cal Poly, he was given a tryout by the Washington Redskins and the Los Angeles Chargers (before they became the San Diego Chargers and then the Los Angeles Chargers again!) as an undrafted rookie. Ironic that he later became the GM for both of those NFL clubs.

When he didn't stick with either team, Bobby didn't want to leave football. Therefore, he took a job in 1963 as a part-time scout for the Kansas City Chiefs.

He then served as a scout for the Atlanta Falcons from 1968 through 1971.

Bobby had a major breakthrough in 1972. That was when he became the Director of Player Personnel for the Miami Dolphins. In that role, he enjoyed the Dolphins' fantastic success of winning the following two Super Bowls.

In 1973, Bobby's players for the Dolphins had a perfect regular season and won the Super Bowl. That feat has not been repeated since.

The Washington Redskins named Bobby their new General Manager in 1978. As the Redskins GM, he helped lead the team to three Super Bowls and two Super Bowl Championships.

Bobby was the consummate judge of football and football coaching talent. As an example, it was Bobby who hired Joe Gibbs, who was then an obscure NFL assistant coach, as the

Redskins Head Coach, in 1981. Joe Gibbs is now in the NFL Hall of Fame.

With Gibbs leading the team, the Redskins subsequently won two Super Bowls in 1982 and 1987.

For the Super Bowl that the Redskins won in San Diego, in 1987, the Redskins Quarterback was Doug Williams.

Doug Williams had been a former No. 1 draft pick of the Tampa Bay Buccaneers. When the Buccaneers gave up on him, Bobby snatched him up for the Redskins. Williams' fabulous Super Bowl performance and victory followed soon thereafter.

Before Bobby left the Redskins, he drafted Mark Rypien in the sixth round in 1986. Rypien went on to win the Super Bowl with the Redskins in 1991. Most of the players on that Super Bowl winning team had been chosen by Bobby.

Two years later, in the 1988 draft, Bobby's last draft for the Redskins, he used the Redskins' sixth-round pick to select Stan Humphries. After Bobby came over to the Chargers, he managed to bring Stan Humphries to the team. Humphries later led the Chargers to their only Super Bowl appearance, against the San Francisco 49ers.

As the Chargers GM, the team won its first division title in more than a decade during his third season and, by his fifth year, they had their only appearance in a Super Bowl in the history of the club.

———

Now, circling back to the question of why Bobby is not in the NFL Hall of Fame. Once again, a quick review: Here's a guy who had a critical role in the Dolphins, Redskins, and Chargers reaching the Super Bowl. Four of those teams won Super Bowls.

After one of the Super Bowl wins by the Redskins, Bobby's picture was on the cover of Sports Illustrated, under the caption: "The Smartest Man in Football."

Bobby's reaction to that title was total embarrassment. He has never been comfortable with that kind of personal attention.

How could it be that the Smartest Man in Football hasn't been selected for the NFL Hall of Fame?

Some people attribute that fact to Bobby selecting Ryan Leaf as the No. 2 draft pick in 1998. Ryan Leaf was one of the legendary busts in NFL history.

The guy Bobby wanted was Peyton Manning, who was taken No. 1 by the Indianapolis Colts. It was later acknowledged by other General Managers around the NFL that they would've taken Leaf as No. 2, if they had been in Bobby's shoes.

Bobby later admitted to me that in taking Ryan Leaf, he violated his cardinal rule that had led him to such great success in his NFL drafting over so many years. He acknowledged that this was the one and only time that he drafted a player without first checking with that player's college team's trainer.

In this case, unfortunately, Bobby was misled by the Washington State Coach, Mike Price, about the quarterback's level of maturity.

Back to the trainer for Washington State. The day after Bobby had drafted Leaf as the No. 2 pick, that trainer called him.

He began the phone conversation by remonstrating to Bobby that Bobby should've called him before the draft. He went on to relate that Ryan was a real head case who had been brought up as the only boy among a huge number of female cousins. As a result, Leaf had been spoiled rotten since he was a kid.

So there you are. The reason Bobby probably isn't in the

NFL Hall of Fame today is that he violated his own ironclad rule of always calling the team's trainer before he drafted any player!

———————

When Bobby left the Chargers, he became a special consultant to the Atlanta Falcons for a couple of years because the owner, Arthur Blank, was such a close friend and wanted to use Bobby's vast NFL football knowledge to help build his team.

Bobby ultimately retired in the year 2000.

———————

Bobby is one of the most competitive people I've ever met. For example, from 2005 to 2009, Bobby won five consecutive titles in the men's age 65 and over group at the World Body Surfing Championships, held annually at the Oceanside Pier.

From his childhood friends, I've heard epic stories about Bobby's indomitable competitiveness over his lifetime. Stories like Bobby taking on trained track runners in track endurance tests and finally running them into the ground.

But I think the one thing that makes Bobby stand out in the professional football world is how highly respected and beloved he is by former football players, coaches, team owners, and various NFL administrators.

I got to see this for myself when I used to accompany Bobby to his GM box at Qualcomm Stadium, during Chargers home games. I was amazed to watch as Bobby was greeted before and after the games by so many people, at so many levels, from the opposing teams.

If the question of Bobby's being placed in the NFL Hall of Fame was posed to everyone connected with the League over the nearly 40 years that Bobby worked in the NFL, I can guarantee he would be a shoo-in, first ballot, Hall of Fame choice.

One last vision of Bobby which, at least in my mind, forever encapsulates the fact that this football icon never left his Southern California beach roots.

After Bobby retired, he spent a couple of years as a football studio analyst with NBC. I don't recall who his fellow panelists were, other than Terry Bradshaw, but it was the usual collection of NFL Hall of Fame football players and coaches.

I was watching one broadcast when, for some reason, the TV cameraman pulled back from the usual close-ups that show the panelists only from the waist up.

By doing so, you could see how the panelists were attired below their beltline. Of course, everyone had on their matching logoed sports jacket and red ties. The rest of the panelists had on dark pants, and highly conservative, well-polished footwear.

However, in that particular shot, Bobby kind of stood out. Instead of having conservative slacks on, he was wearing chinos. And when it came to footwear, he apparently didn't get the network memo.

He was wearing a pair of beat up topsiders with no socks!

My kind of guy!

NFL Hall of Fame update: Finally, the Hall's electors got it right. Bobby recently was selected for the NFL Hall of Fame.

Bobby, your buddies in the Tuesday Morning Gang salute you! It's about time!

- three -

Roy Bream

It's now time to discuss the life of one of the founders of the Tuesday Morning Gang, the peripatetic story of Roy Bream.

As I've noted elsewhere, there is some internal disagreements among the members concerning the origin of this august body. However, Roy and Skip are most comfortable with the version of the two of them first getting together in the 1990s at the Pannikin in Leucadia and at Cardiff Seaside Market.

At some later time, within the next couple of years, Bobby Beathard, Woody Ekstrom, and his brother Carl, happened to run across Skip and Roy when they were having coffee together, and they ended up joining the gang. Thus we had the momentous initial merger of the South Bay and Windansea contingents.

In keeping with his nomadic lifestyle, Roy is presently up on the Central Coast of California, seeking a position as the Interim City Manager for the City of Morro Bay. While he is applying for that position, he is serving in a PR capacity and working on security at the Hearst Castle.

Roy's family history started in Scotland.

In an interesting migratory route from Scotland to Canada, and then on to Manhattan Beach in the South Bay, Roy's granddad and family settled in Manhattan Beach in 1921.

Roy is a true-blue South Bay guy, having been born in the Torrance Hospital and living in a number of homes in Manhattan Beach and Hermosa Beach until he went away to college.

At Mira Costa High School, Rory was a wrestler and played basketball. He also had the distinction, which he shared with Dewey Weber, of being the shortest members of their freshman and sophomore classes. Whenever they were asked to line up according to height, he and Dewey were always at the end of the line.

Roy was involved as a friend and companion of some of the original surf icons, such as Dewey Weber, Bing Copeland, Greg Knoll, Hap Jacobs, and Dale Velzy.

Roy reminisced with me about observing Dale Velzy shaping his first surfboards under the Manhattan Beach pier, until Velzy was run off by the authorities. Roy stated that Dale next opened a tiny shop about a block away from the pier where he first began selling his surfboards.

Roy first met Bobby Beathard when Bobby was going to El Segundo High School and Roy was at Mira Costa.

Roy began lifeguarding with the LA County lifeguards in 1957, when he was 18. He and Bobby worked together as lifeguards at 22nd Street in Hermosa Beach.

Over the years, Roy worked as a seasonal lifeguard for some

10 years. While he was in the lifeguard service, he competed on numerous lifeguard national teams.

I'm not sure what years Roy won the Catalina to Manhattan Beach Pier paddle board contest, but according to the *Surfer's Journal*, he was a multiple year winner.

As one of the pre-eminent paddlers of his time, Roy managed to become the much envied owner of a storied paddle board made by Joe Quigg – one of only three iconic paddle boards that were produced by Quigg during the 1950s. Those Quigg paddleboards are considered the Holy Grail for paddlers.

When Roy was 18, he had one of his first run-ins with the formidable Howard Bugbee.

At the time, Roy had tried out for Howard's paddling team and become a member. The team was sponsored by Howard, through the Poop Deck, and was called the Blackhawks. Apparently they were quite successful in paddleboard competitions.

After one of their victories, Roy, who had never before been in the Poop Deck, at least not drinking, decided that it was time to put on his big boy pants and belly up to the bar with the other paddlers.

That plan went quite smoothly until the ever-vigilant Howard spied the 18-year-old Roy Bream standing at the bar.

Once again, as had been the case with Tommy Dunne, and probably other underaged members of our esteemed group, in spite of Roy being one of Howard's team's victorious paddlers, Howard promptly threw Roy's fanny out into the street!

Since Roy's resume didn't indicate when he served in the Coast Guard, I guess this is as good a place as any to cover his military service.

Roy stated that when he received a very official looking letter from the US Government, having a strong aversion to receiving bad news, Roy tossed the letter aside.

At the time Roy, was hanging out with a bunch of older guys. He said that during that era, the younger surfer types usually hung out at 22nd Street, while the "old surfers," those who were 5 to 10 years older than the kids, hung out at 21st Street.

One day Roy decided to bring the unopened letter down to 21st Street so he could discuss it with some of the more experienced, older surfer dudes.

One of them finally opened the letter and actually read what it said. With great trepidation, Roy inquired of the reader about the letter's contents.

Roy was told that it wasn't an induction notice into the military. However, it was a notice that induction was imminent!

Not being particularly interested in the potential enjoyment of the sights and sounds of the Vietnamese jungle, replete with booby-traps and fanatical opposition troops, Roy plaintively inquired of his more experienced buddies what he should do.

To a man, the advice was all the same. Follow in the footsteps of Howard Bugbee, Woody Ekstrom, and Pat O'Connor, and beat feet to the nearest US Coast Guard recruiting office.

Not wanting to wait for the arrival of the next very serious letter from the US government, marking his induction, Roy immediately followed his buddies' advice and enlisted in the Coast Guard at Long Beach.

Roy did not serve out his two years. After he had been in for about a year, he took advantage of a new program where he could go into the US Coast Guard Reserves and, with credit for his previous service, immediately leave the active duty ranks.

After that, he served six more years in the Reserves, attending monthly meetings.

When Roy finished telling me about his Coast Guard career, why did it not surprise me when he candidly acknowledged to me that he wasn't really cut out to be in the military!?

Getting back to Roy's education, when Roy started college he initially matriculated at Orange Coast Junior College.

According to Roy, he went there so he could learn how to sail!

While surfing in the Orange County area, he ran into Hobie Alter. He told Hobie that he was looking for a roommate. Hobie suggested Joey Cabell. At the time, Joey had just won the big Makaha surfing contest, which at that time was the equivalent of the world surfing championship.

Once the two of them got together as roomies, it was the beginning of the lengthy relationship. While they were roommates, in addition to surfing, they also spent a lot of time skiing together.

His roommate, Joey, got together with Buzzy Bent, and they opened the first Chart House on July 4, 1961, in Aspen, Colorado.

Later on, Roy was the General Manager of that Chart House restaurant from 1971 to 1976.

––––––––

The next college stop for Roy was Santa Barbara City College. Roy shared with me that he chose to go to that school in order to have more time for his surfing!

Are we developing a pattern here?

Next up for Roy was USC for his final two years of college. Since the ocean isn't particularly close to the school, I have to assume that he decided that it was time for him to focus on his education, and at least almost as much as his surfing and sailing.

However, he did manage to spend some time on the water because he rowed on the crew team for his last two years at USC.

In 1964, Roy graduated from USC with a Bachelor of Science in Business Administration, with a major in Marketing.

––––––––

After graduating from USC in 1964, Roy went back up to Santa Barbara to work as a yacht broker for a year.

Fortuitously, Roy next met Jim Kilroy, at that time a relatively new developer. He worked as a Vice President and partner with Kilroy Industries Inc. in Los Angeles, from 1964 through 1971.

Kilroy's company went on to become a very major developer in Southern California. As a matter of fact, they are huge developers in San Diego County, including the ginormous project that they are trying to get approved in San Diego at this writing, One Paseo.

During his work with Kilroy, Roy got married and he and his wife lived in Hollywood.

———————

Roy also got to indulge in one of his favorite pastimes while working with Kilroy; sailing. He and Jim Kilroy sailed together for 12 years, including a number of Transpacs and TransAtlantic races.

As I noted earlier, Roy left his position with Kilroy and then became the General Manager of the Chart House in Aspen.

———————

Then Roy "pulled a Bream." The resume Roy sent to me indicated his next job was in Houston, Texas, as the lead diver for International Divers Inc.! He held this job from 1976 to 1979.

There are career changes which are relatively normal segues. But this one, other than the fact that it involved water, has left me totally stymied!

What I want to know is how and why in heaven's name did Roy go from greeting customers at the Chart House in Aspen, to wandering around the bottom of the ocean with a bell helmet on his head?!

———————

The pull of California got Roy back to his old stomping grounds in Santa Barbara, California, from 1979 to 1984.

In that city, he was the founder and President of a company operating supply vessels, crew boats, dredges and tugboats in the

United States, Puerto Rico and Africa, primarily serving offshore gas, oil, and construction companies.

Well, at least Roy's career segue this time was a little more logical than the one from running a Chart House to becoming a lead commercial diver!

Roy's next move was from tugboats to men's sportswear manufacturing. So what else would you expect when Roy Bream was doing a career course correction?

From 1984 to 1986, he was the President and Chief Operating Officer for Norfleet Hawaii, Inc., in Irvine California. The company was involved in wholesale men's sportswear manufacturing.

In 1986, Roy returned to his Chart House roots. From 1986 to 1997 he worked with Chart House Enterprises Inc., and subsidiaries, in Solana Beach. While with the company, he was the President/Chief Operating Officer/Director of Paradise Bakery, a subsidiary of the Chart House. Later he was promoted to Vice President/Real Estate and Development, and then to Senior Vice President of Chart House Enterprises Inc.

In his more than a decade's worth of work for the Chart House, he had a variety of assignments. They included: site acquisitions and dispositions; negotiations with City, County and State agencies to obtain permits and approvals; and, design and construction of Chart House and Islands restaurants, and Paradise Bakeries, throughout the US.

His work also included operating responsibility for dozens of company-owned restaurants, in addition to directing franchise operations. Roy was actually involved in the restructuring of the Paradise Bakery & Café into a franchise operation.

There's a lot more, but it might be easier for you to ask Roy for a copy of his resume! I'm running out of titles and job descriptions!

In 1997 Roy returned to his love for sailing.

During his adult life, Roy has been involved in just about every type of ocean racing known to man. His sailboat racing has included serving on the crew of the last two Kings of Norway!

When Roy dropped that little pearl in his resume, obviously your intrepid reporter had to pursue that story.

Turns out that because of his reputation in international sailboat racing, in 1984 Roy was asked by King Olav, then the King of Norway, to crew on his 5.5 m racing sailboat.

Whenever King Olav entered his boat in a sailboat race up until 1991, Roy would receive word that he was invited to crew for those races.

King Olav died in January 1991. His son, Harald then became King.

Assuming his dad's Crown wasn't the only hereditary passage from King Olav to King Harald. The new King also inherited Roy Bream as a crew member on his 5.5 m racing boat!

Since then, Roy has crewed for King Harald whenever he races his sailboat.

Roy shared with me that whenever he does show up in Norway

to crew for the King, he has a few weeks of living like a king himself.

For example, he gets to attend banquets at the King's side and goes through massive ceremonial receiving lines as the number two person of the honorees, directly behind the King. Roy even stated that when the maître d' comes up to the King to indicate that the desserts are ready to be served, once again the King goes first, followed closely by our own Roy Bream.

Exercising my usual discrete literary restraint, I didn't ask Roy whether he had ever enjoyed any successful trolling (in a nautical manner of speaking, of course), among the lovely Norwegian ladies while he was accompanying the King.

Sorry, but it's time for Roy to return to the more mundane everyday task of earning a living.

From 1997 to 2005, Roy was the president of Swan Pacific LLC, in Newport Beach. With that company, he was the exclusive agent for the Nautor Swan sailing yachts for the Southwestern US.

The Swan sailboats are manufactured by a company in Finland. They are world-class sailboats and racing yachts.

In 2005 Roy moved to San Diego where he has had a variety of positions, including yacht broker and consultant.

He then moved up to the Central California Coast where he now resides.

Time to wrap up Roy's story, but I'm having difficulty getting my head around how to summarize such a fascinating and varied life.

Maybe Chris Aherns did the best job in an article about Roy in the *Coast News* which I read, but unfortunately can't find again.

Chris was attempting to encapsulate Roy's life at the present time. The way he put it was that on any given day you might see Roy paddling his version of the Holy Grail, Joe Quigg's 18-foot balsawood paddleboard, racing along just beyond the surfline.

Or, as Chris envisioned it, that day you might see Roy speeding by on his bike on Coast Highway 101.

In the alternative, Roy might sail by in a beautiful Swan 66 sailboat as he skippers the yacht in a demonstration for a potential buyer.

Or finally, if the surf's up, Roy could be taking the point break, riding one of Donald Takayama's noseriders for a run at the Cardiff Reef.

———

Chris Ahrens did a nice job describing Roy's life. However, he left out a part that Chris may not have known about. That part of Roy's life that the members of our august body are quite familiar with.

We have to be quiet about this part. Everyone is sworn to secrecy!

Two of our members (that would be Yuma Bill and Roy) have something in common. The commonality is that they are both interminably searching for sweet young things who have grandfather fetishes!

- four -

Howard Bugbee

I'm really excited this morning. I finally got to talk to Howard long enough so that I could get sufficient background info on his extraordinarily colorful history to start writing this biography. I've been bugging Howard and Eileen for this background information to the point where I'm surprised they even take my phone calls anymore.

Of course to be fair, with all the time that Howard has been spending recently in hospitals and rehab facilities, maybe I am a bit of a pest with my target fixation on this anthology project . . . YAH THINK?

Fortunately, Howard decided to call me this morning.

Sadly, the reason for his call was to report a new hospitalization, and his present renewed incarceration at a rehab facility.

Interestingly enough, Eileen just commented to me that it's much easier to have Howard home, rather than in rehab. She's much more comfortable with the rhythm of their lives while at home, than commuting to the rehab facility every day.

The good news is that Howard likes this rehab facility. He had a pleasant prior experience there.

According to Eileen, who I talked with immediately after

my phone conversation with Howard, at this facility you can eat anything you want, whenever you want it. Given mostly tasteless institutional fare, that arrangement would do wonders for most anyone's attitude!

———

Unfortunately for Howard and Eileen, his primary caregiver and Guardian Angel (not to mention the members of the Tuesday Morning Gang who all care so much for Howard and Eileen), we've all lost track of how many times Howard has been hospitalized and in rehab over the last few years.

But regardless of his incredible series of medical issues, The Good Ship Howard Bugbee (aided by his indomitable first mate, Eileen), keeps merrily sailing along. Howard does so with an unbowed attitude and a grim determination to battle his way back through these tempestuous medical seas, to achieve decent health again.

———

So let's get on with the fascinating story of Howard's extraordinary life, shall we.

Howard was originally brought up in Los Angeles. During the summer, his dad would bring the family down to spend a week or two in Manhattan Beach. During those summer vacations, the family would enjoy staying in houses along the beach.

In 1940, Howard's dad had a home built in the northern portion of Manhattan Beach.

I asked Howard when he first began spending time in Hermosa Beach. He related that, as a kid, he used to ride his bike or take the bus down to Hermosa Beach, where he had a bunch of buddies. They would all get together and hang out on 13th Street.

Howard remembers that he and his buddies were not favorites of the local gendarmes. The reason was that, to the policemen's ever evolving displeasure, Howard and the gang took great delight in periodically jumping off of the Hermosa Beach pier.

Although he was a little unclear on this point during our phone conversation, I believe that Howard and some of his friends may have been apprehended by the police for jumping from the pier on December 7, 1941, "the day which will live in infamy!"

That day also happened to be Howard's birthday!

Howard related to me that he attended the "really old" Redondo High School because that was the only high school at the time serving students in the South Bay. His initial attendance at Redondo was before the new Mira Costa High School was built.

When I asked Howard what sports he played in high school, his quick response was "all of them." He said that the school was packed with outstanding athletes. As an example, he named Frank Gifford as one of the athletes who was prominent in the area at the time.

However, in spite of Howard's general love of all sports, his primary emphasis was on the football and track teams in high school.

While Howard was still in high school, he ran a 9.6 second 100-yard dash and a 220-yard sprint in 21 seconds!

For those of you who are not track aficionados, you have to trust me when I tell you that, even today, those would still be extremely fast times for a California high school sprinter, almost 70 years later!

Because of his athletic prowess, Howard managed to get a scholarship offer from Stanford to play football. Howard played as a half back on the only freshman football team in the history of Stanford to go undefeated.

The team included Bill McCall, who had a storied football career at Stanford. I even remember reading about Mr. McCall in the sports pages, way back when I was a kid on the East Coast. McCall went on to enjoy an eight year run in the NFL, playing for the Chicago Bears, until he left the league to go back to medical school.

Another one of Howard's friends at Redondo High School, Mickey Colmar, was such a great football player as a kid that Howard reported that the legendary George Halas, the owner of the Bears, came all the way to California to scout Colmar when he was still in high school!

Things were going swimmingly for Howard during his freshman year at Stanford – at least until shortly after the end of the football season.

At this juncture I have to make an admission. From all the stories and legends about Howard, I had always assumed that he went from high school directly to USC, and turned into a collegiate track superstar.

When I was talking with Eileen a few weeks ago, I mentioned that fact.

Her quick and rather emphatic response was: "Nope Charley. Howard started college at Stanford, not USC!"

Initially I thought she was pulling my leg. How could all of this carefully nurtured collegiate lore about Howard be so wrong?

When I questioned her on the unexpected news, she had her typical Eileen direct, and very much to the point, reply.

> "Charley, he was only at Stanford for the first quarter of his freshman year. At the end of the football season, he water bombed the Dean of the College and the administration threw him out of the hallowed halls. It was after he got thrown out of Stanford that he was admitted to USC!"

I'm not sure how anybody else would've reacted to that shocking piece of information about our hero, Howard.

Personally however, I didn't vacillate at all. I was overjoyed to receive the news!!

In my twisted mind, this was the kind of escapade that could only enhance the already storied legend of the life of Howard Bugbee!!

———

So how did Howard's budding collegiate career so suddenly careen off the tracks?

Well, you have Eileen's version. And on the other hand, you have Howard's version.

As I noted above, Eileen's version was that Howard managed to nail the Stanford Dean with the water bomb. I actually like her story a lot better than Howard's, because in her version Howard exhibits considerably more panache!

According to Howard, it didn't happen exactly that way. He had a buddy by the name of Dick Wall who had a dorm room, which I believe Howard indicated was on the fourth-story of the building, above a campus snack shop.

For afternoon entertainment, Howard and Mr. Wall would drop water bombs on the unsuspecting students, as they were exiting or entering the snack shop. Again, according to Howard's version, unfortunately somebody ratted them out and the two of them were tossed out of the school.

I'm a little confused about the duration of the Stanford administered punishment. I believe that Howard indicated that he was supposed to be suspended from attending Stanford for a school quarter, but I can't swear by that. It's academic anyway, because Howard, exhibiting laser focus and no interest in dilly-dallying, decided to immediately transfer to Stanford's archrival, USC.

In any event, I'm sure that by now the reader can understand why I prefer Eileen's version of this little college diversion! I mean think of all of the additional points that you earn by nailing the college Dean, as opposed to just some everyday students!

———

Fortunately, we're going to eventually be able to straighten this out. Howard's story will be vetted by Eileen and him, not to mention by the hundreds of fact checkers that I've employed at great expense, just to make certain that you guys are not pulling my chain about your personal histories.

Total transparency is our motto here!

In any event, to Howard's good fortune, USC stayed true to its primary collegiate mission of producing world-class athletes. No sooner had he been tossed out of Stanford on his backside, than Howard was welcomed with open arms at USC!

Oops!! I stand corrected!

I just got off the phone with Howard and he told me that there was a 13-month hiatus between his being run out of Palo Alto on a rail and commencing his collegiate run at USC.

So what does a young man do after being politely escorted to the exit from a prestigious university?

As just related to me by Howard, the answer is that one goes out and becomes a tuna fisherman, that's what one does!

Howard's dad apparently had some connections within the Port of San Diego tuna industry. He managed to get Howard a crewman's spot on board one of the long-ranging tuna seiners of that era.

They went off on a 63-day fishing voyage. They fished for tuna off the Galapagos Islands and the coast of Costa Rica.

During the trip they had multiple crossings of the equator. For those of you who are not familiar with nautical traditions, it's customary for fellow crew members to put newbies to the equator crossing through initiation rites.

In Howard's case, he was given a free Mohawk haircut!

You've all seen still and moving pictures of these tuna fishermen in action. Once the seiner gets in the middle of a bait ball, the fisherman toss their lines out into the middle of the boil with a jig. Since the tuna are in a feeding frenzy, they'll hit anything that attracts their attention.

I asked Howard a question that has always bothered me when I watch these old tuna fishing movies. What's the trick in getting the tuna off the jig, after the fisherman has flipped that big old sucker back over his shoulder into the bowels of the ship?

Howard answered that it's simple. When the fishing line goes slack, the jig slips right out of the tuna's mouth.

Howard stated that on some occasions he was asked to man two fishing rigs at the same time. Frankly, I can't imagine how that would be done.

———

Howard explained that there was usually about a 15-man crew of fisherman on their long-range tuna seiner, in addition to the cooks. He also indicated that it was a very diverse group, including some Portuguese, as well as a number of Japanese fishermen.

———

According to Howard, they had a very successful fishing trip. I believe that he said that they had 293 tons of tuna on board when they came back to San Diego to the processing plant.

———

In true Howard Bugbee fashion, pursuing his bachelor's degree did not exactly involve a linear run for his diploma from USC.

We were a little vague on the timing this morning, but basically it is my understanding that Howard took a bit of a detour while he was matriculating at USC by doing a stint in the US Coast Guard.

———

Howard's logic behind suddenly leaping at the opportunity to ensure the safeguarding of our country's shores was impeccable.

It was either that, or he was going to be subjected to induction in the US Army. He would then be scheduled to receive a totally insufficient and brief training regime at a US Army boot camp before the Army, in its infinite wisdom, shipped him off to Korea to freeze his ass off, all the while fighting off masses of rampaging North Korean and Chinese soldiers!

This Hobson's choice came about in this fashion. Howard's local draft office advised him that he was about to become one of the 80,000 per month reluctant and very involuntary draftees who were being scarfed up by the US Army, preparatory to their ill-fated shipment across the Pacific to the Korean Peninsula.

Demonstrating wisdom well beyond his years, Howard temporarily bailed on his USC collegiate career, and using his world-class speed, he beat feet over to the US Coast Guard recruiting office lickety-split!

This is not a matter of common knowledge. However other than being stationed at Kodiak, Alaska, as my cousin was (he was properly rewarded for that hellish tour of duty by ultimately retiring from the Coast Guard as a Vice Admiral!), ending up at various Coast Guard stations around the world is generally pretty damn good duty!

Howard's experience was not an exception to that rule. As a

matter of fact, one of his favorite duty stations was working at the Palos Verdes lighthouse where they had six hours on duty, and six hours off.

Think Howard managed to squeeze in a little surfing time during that crushing duty assignment?

Not only that, but because of Howard's duty schedule at the lighthouse, according to Eileen, he often was able to go home and have his mother fix him his lunch!

Options like having my mom who lived in Connecticut prepare lunch for me were not available when I was in the US Navy, stationed on Guam, out in the middle of the Pacific Ocean!

Rumor has it that Howard was not the most motivated fellow ever to serve in the US Coast Guard. As a matter of fact, he managed to earn a certain reputation while a member of that esteemed service.

He actually earned a nickname which was derived from Howard's less than stellar attitude toward carrying out his Coast Guard duties.

Howard, never one to try to hide his opinions, had a well-earned reputation for constantly carrying on among his ship-mates about his objections to the personal indignities that he was being subjected to as a Coast Guard Seaman.

Thus the sobriquet of "Bitchbee" was added by his ship-mates, in front of his surname, Bugbee. As in good old Bitchbee Bugbee!

Although I'm not certain about the timing, at some point Howard was kidnapped by the US Navy from the Coast Guard and sent back to Annapolis, Maryland, to train as a sprinter for the Olympics.

In talking with Howard, he confirmed that he trained for both the 1952 and the 1956 Olympics.

Eileen said that Howard and some of his buddies used to jump on a train when they had weekend leave and run up to Harlem in New York for entertainment. *[I don't doubt there are some wild stories in that portion of Howard's history!]*

I was trying to imagine how, back during that era, Howard and his other lily white Olympics trainee buddies could just go marching into Harlem, without being accompanied by an extensive group of armed guards.

On the phone just now, Howard offered an explanation of why they had the temerity to pop into the Harlem nightclubs.

As related by Howard, there were a couple of world-class black athletes who were training along with them in Annapolis. These two individuals would serve as their advance guard and scouting party for their forays into Harlem.

———

Sadly, in Annapolis, where Howard was training, they had a banked indoor track. Because the weather is always perfect in Southern California, Howard was not accustomed to doing his running on a banked indoor track.

That led to a serious injury to one of Howard's legs. He severely pulled a muscle in the leg. Eileen contends that even today, he still sports a rather prominent depression where the injury occurred.

———

In any event, Howard's performances as a USC track athlete were legendary.

In college he ran a 9.5 second 100-yard dash and a best 220 time (I believe that the distances were changed to 100m and 200m at a later date) of 20.8.

Once again campers, we're looking at some bodaciously fast sprint times here!

As a matter of fact, Howard and his fellow 4 X 200 (220 yard) sprint relay team members at USC came within one-tenth of a second of the world's sprint relay record for that distance. I think their USC time for the 4 x 100 sprint relay was something like 40.5 seconds . . . incredibly fast back in those days.

Howard is still grousing about coming so close, without breaking the world record. As he explained it in no uncertain terms to me this morning, their sprint relay anchorman was dogging it on the final leg!

———

Now we get to the good part of Howard's career, as the impresario of the legendary Hermosa Beach dive joint, the Poop Deck.

Because of his stint in the Coast Guard, Howard wasn't exactly still a kid when he graduated from USC in 1956. In fact, he was in his mid-20s.

Ever the entrepreneur, with the Poop Deck, Howard managed to come up with a new business enterprise which he virtually created out of whole cloth.

In Hermosa Beach, Howard noted that a "joint" (Howard's words), called Tortilla Flats, had recently been shut down. It was

Howard's impression that they had had a successful business, but skimmed off the money and took off for parts unknown.

Howard immediately liked the location.

The space they had occupied was not exactly gigantic. As a matter of fact, it only measured 15 feet across!

Howard made the obvious decision that he needed to widen the facility, and eventually the Poop Deck's width was doubled and it became 30 feet wide.

Howard was not exactly bucks up when he originally opened the Poop Deck. In fact, he had to sell his car and borrow money from two friends in order to raise the capital necessary to start the new business venture.

―――――――

During the approximately 10 years that Howard owned the Poop Deck, I've been told that it became the dive joint of choice for most of the discerning party people in the South Bay. Howard mentioned that it was a particular favorite of surfers and lifeguards.

I know that all of the members of our group who originally came from the South Bay speak about the Poop Deck reverently, as if it served as their home away from home.

Howard related to me that he ran a very tight ship when it came to adhering to the existing rules and regulations, particularly those relating to his ABC liquor license.

He indicated that he had some competition that would've been delighted to see him lose his liquor license, so he had to be extremely diligent in that regard.

So diligent that among our own membership, people like Tommy Dunne still bitch and moan (believe it or not almost 60 years after the fact, I might note!) about how unfriendly Howard was back then, throwing their underage backsides out of his drinking emporium, into the street.

Even today, Howard's steadfast response to these complaints receive the back of his hand. As Howard put it:

> "Why in the hell should I have let you underage punks, who never paid for any liquor in my establishment because all you did was mooch beers off my real customers, jeopardize my liquor license for such a bunch of miscreants (the word actually used by Howard was well off the charts of the profanity spectrum, but, once again, a reminder that we're PG rated here)!"

———

Speaking of Tommy Dunne, Eileen shared a story with me this morning that made me chuckle. Apparently Tommy and his wife initially met at the Poop Deck. I have to assume that it was during the period of Howard's proprietorship.

Eileen commented that ever since their first meeting there, Howard's old dive joint has had a very significant place in their hearts. As a matter of fact, she reported that they celebrated their 50th wedding anniversary at the Poop Deck, before the good ship was decommissioned.

[As an aside, I can't tell you how hard it is for me not to make a smartass remark at this point about Tommy and his wife's concept of a romantic setting. However, I'm going to overcome my normal predilection and just not go there . . .]

Howard sold the Poop Deck in the mid-1960s. This became a financial necessity because of Howard's divorce from his first wife.

Then Howard opened up a new beer/wine bar called the Blue Book in El Portal, further inland.

Howard ran that facility for four years and then sold it.

His next business venture was back in Hermosa Beach when he opened the High Seas Bar. According to Howard, this was a former gay bar that he converted into a straight bar.

Some of the old customers of the previous establishment weren't too happy about the conversion and gave Howard a hard time. As a matter fact, being particularly bad sports about the matter, they apparently made a concerted effort to have Howard's liquor license taken away from him.

One other Howard story about the High Seas Bar before we move on.

Howard related to me that one day he was just lounging in the bar on a real quiet afternoon. A gentleman who seemed to have a very agreeable personality joined him at his table. They had a great conversation that went on for some time.

That was the good aspect of the meeting.

The not so good part was the manner of the gentleman's departure from Howard's company.

After their very comfortable conversation, during which

Howard undoubtedly identified who he was, the gentleman hesitated before he walked out of the bar.

Then he suddenly turned toward Howard and handed him Howard's divorce papers!

In other words, Howard had spent a good period of time chatting with a process server who had come into the bar with the specific intent of serving Howard with the divorce papers that had been filed by his soon to be ex-wife!

Now, upon occasion, Howard has been reputed to take extraordinary physical action when aggravated. In this case, apparently he was too shocked to deck the idiot.

[Unlike a good friend of mine: My buddy, upon answering a knock at the front door of his home after the visitor told a bald-faced lie about the purpose of his visit, was served with a lawsuit. Without hesitating, my friend coldcocked the lying SOB. That might've been the end of the matter if the California State Bar hadn't taken umbrage at my friend's reaction in the form of disciplinary action relating to his license to practice law.]

———

I just got off the phone with Eileen and she told me the story about how she and Howard first got together. It's such a classic Howard story that I've immediately run back to my computer to try to memorialize the details of that event, before I suffer my normal memory collapse that my advancing years continue to bestow upon me.

———

Eileen related that they originally got together on the beach at Waikiki, at the very posh and exclusive Outrigger Club.

Already sounds pretty romantic, doesn't it?

Wait for it . . . I guess the answer to that question is all in the eyes of the beholder.

The way their initial encounter developed, went along these lines.

That afternoon, apparently Howard, along with a bunch of his buddies, for the first time took on Makaha, where 12-foot boomers were breaking.

According to Eileen, after this fantastic surfing nirvana event had occurred, Howard and the guys all piled back into their van and began driving over to Waikiki.

Along the way, in their absolute exuberance, Howard and his buddies may have overindulged in the wicked weed. Eileen related that their van was undoubtedly the Doobie Express, all the way back across the island to Waikiki!

In the meantime, Eileen and one of her stewardess friends were enjoying a relaxed, quiet afternoon, laying out on the beach in the sedate and private environment of the world-famous Outrigger Club.

Eileen specifically remembered that four elderly friends of hers, all in their 80s, were quietly playing bridge at a table close to where she and her friend were sunning themselves on the beach.

––––––––

Suddenly this serene luxurious club scene was obscenely violated by the obstreperous and loud arrival of Howard and his equally stoned friends.

Before she knew it, Eileen found Howard lying in the sand next to her and doing his damnedest, given his severely mind-altered condition, to carry on a conversation with her.

The first indication that Eileen had that all was not totally well with Howard's person at that particular moment was when he did a very normal thing; he asked Eileen for her name. Eileen told him.

So far so good. However, only moments later, he once again politely asked Eileen what her name was. Once again, Eileen told Howard her name.

Moments later Eileen was a little disturbed when he asked her for a third time what her name was, as Howard acknowledged that he was having a little difficulty remembering the answer.

Eileen indicated to me that at this juncture in their initial "conversation," all she could think about was how the hell she was going to get away from this idiot!

Sadly for the decorum of this world-renowned private club, Howard was not quite ready to quietly depart the premises.

———————

By this point in the proceedings, Howard had total target fixation on Eileen.

He started asking her for her phone number so that they could get together later. She replied that her social calendar was pretty well slammed, so there was no point in exchanging phone numbers.

Eileen did acknowledge to me that she was dating multiple guys at that time. Given, in their initial encounter, Howard's managing to so successfully come across as such a crushing bore, Eileen decided that she had no inclination whatsoever to even consider adding Howard to her burgeoning stable of potential dates.

Subsequent events during the next hour or so did absolutely nothing to change Eileen's negative first impressions of our buddy Howard!

———

Not to be deterred, Howard then began ragging on Eileen's friend in an effort to elicit Eileen's phone number from her. With that development, Eileen gave her friend strict instructions not to share, under any circumstances whatsoever, that state secret with Howard, upon penalty of death or dismemberment!

Well I want to tell you that when Howard gets target fixation, it's an awesome spectacle to behold!

In Eileen's mind, what followed next absolutely cemented her decision to remove herself as far as possible away from this crazy individual.

Eileen got up and tried to leave. Suffice it to say, Howard did not get the hint.

Not only did he not get the hint, but he tackled her!

You can imagine the elderly ladies sitting at their bridge table, totally aghast at the outlandish antics of this unwanted interloper into their posh sanctum.

But fasten your seatbelts, ladies, it's only going to get worse!

After tackling her, once Howard had Eileen supine in the sand again, he started sucking on her toes!!

Eileen, and everyone else who was suffering through the discomfort of being present in that area at the time, were appalled by Howard's blatant public demonstration of his full-blown foot fetish!

———

Fortunately for the fair maiden in such dire distress, Eileen was finally able to extract herself from Howard's amorous clutches and make a hasty retreat, stage left.

But the nightmare wasn't over for Eileen. One of her friends ratted her out and committed the unpardonable sin of giving the ever-persistent Howard, Eileen's phone number.

For days, Howard called Eileen, and called her, and then, called her some more, unerringly maneuvering to get a date with her.

Eileen made an admirable effort to hold out against Howard's relentless blandishments. However, she finally gave in.

One of the pilots she was dating was out of town for a few days, so she finally relented. However, she informed Howard of her agreement to the date under one condition: one and done! In other words, one date and they were finished forever and ever!

———

At the time Eileen had a home in the hills above Waikiki.

At the appointed time, Howard, in Eileen's words, "swaggered" up to her front door.

He made his appearance well-armed. He had a bottle of wine in one hand and a doobie in the other!

Not being one to mess around with the usual social formalities, Howard immediately grabbed Eileen on the front doorstep, embraced her, and gave her a huge kiss.

After finally coming up for air and beating him back, Eileen emphatically told Howard that his conduct was totally unacceptable and that they were going to immediately go to dinner. Then she was going to return home . . . without Howard!

———

Eileen then had to rather sheepishly acknowledge that, as is his custom, Howard had extreme difficulty following her very clear instructions.

In Eileen's final summation, long story short, Howard finally left Eileen's home three days later.

And the rest, as they say, is history . . .

———————

During our phone conversation, Howard and I tried to reconstruct the original organizational genesis of our Tuesday Morning Gang. That's a fancy way of saying how the hell did this all get started!?

In other words, how did this NGO (nongovernmental organization)/nonprofit/nonsensical/etc. etc. group, come into being?

I've run that question by Howard and Roy. I also asked Skip about it.

Howard thinks that it all started back in the 1980s when a bunch of guys used to get together and play sand football on Sunday mornings, at 7th and Strand, in Manhattan Beach.

As Howard recalls it, the original participants, among others who came and went, including some NFL football players, were Howard, Bobby Beathard, Bobby's brother, Pete, both O'Hara brothers (Howard mentioned that Michael O'Hara was a big mucky-muck relative to the 1980 LA Olympics), and occasionally, our very own fearless leader, Skip.

Howard states that Bobby Beathard insisted on their playing sand football on the basis that it would neutralize Howard's world-class speed.

On the other hand, Roy Bream remembers that he and Skip first started to get together much later down at the Cardiff

Seaside Market in the mid-1990s. On rainy days, they would head North up to the Pannikin in Leucadia.

That's also Skip's recollection.

Roy went on to report that later on, in about 1997, they were joined by Carl and Woody Ekstrom, which ultimately led to the formation of the axis of evil between the Windansea and Hermosa Beach surf gangs!

Subsequently, Howard, Mike Burner, Bobby, Tommy Dunne, Clarkie, Pat O'Connor, Tommy Carroll, Jim Enright, Tom Keck, and your humble writer joined the surfing cohort.

The group later expanded again with the addition of Jim Thompson and Yuma Bill Taggart, along with periodic visits by Doug Trenton.

Most recently, Chuck Lindsay has demonstrated a marked lack of societal skills by voluntarily deciding to become an additional member of our motley crew!

Hopefully, over time, that brief history will be subject to the inclusion of much more detail as we check among the ever more elusive memories of the members of our fabled group.

Before I wrap up this brief narrative about Howard's life, I would be remiss if I didn't acknowledge and, upon behalf of the entire Tuesday Morning Gang, thank Eileen for her incredible loving care of our buddy Howard, through so many intractable medical travails.

Over the last few years we've watched in awe as Eileen has taken care of herself and her own very serious medical issues, only after first completely administering to Howard's continuing medical needs.

Among a myriad of other challenging medical conditions, Eileen has been there helping Howard get through his bouts with cancer and an incredible 31-day coma following a less than successful back surgery. Upon numerous occasions, his son, the orthopedic surgeon, Billy Bugbee (an honorary member of our group because he's operated on so many of our gang and their family members) has apparently commented to Eileen that anybody other than his father would've been long gone by this time.

Eileen has dealt with her own battle with the big C and other recent medical challenges, after she has first attended to Howard's outsized medical needs.

And the beauty of Eileen is that she's never lost her sense of humor. No matter how rough the going has gotten, and we all know that it has been incredibly difficult at times, Eileen has always had a smile and a ready wisecrack about dealing with Howard and her latest medical train wreck.

Our hats are off to you ma'am!

As Howard recently acknowledged to me, he definitely got it right the third time around. Their 42 years together has clearly demonstrated to him that Eileen is definitely a keeper!!

-five -

Mike Burner

[Mike Burner prepared his own bio, with a few edits by me.]

Born November 14, 1944, in San Diego. Raised in San Diego County. Moved from Santee to Pacific Beach in 1949 – the best move my parents made, from a chicken ranch in the country to the beach.

I started surfing in the summer of 1958 on a 9'10" balsa wood board made from wood from a WWII life raft – small pieces that were glued together. I bought it from someone in the Navy for $25 that I had earned from my paper route.

I hung out at Al Nelson's surfboard shop – that was just a small garage wherever he could find a place. Pat Curren shaped for Al and shaped my first new surfboard out of balsa wood. I bought it unglassed for $60 and was going to glass it myself (I didn't want to spend $10 to have Ronald Patterson glass it). Pat said "don't screw it up" – but I did. I glassed it outside in my backyard and left it outside overnight to dry. The fog came in and turned the resin a milky color.

I went to Mission Bay High School and graduated in 1962.

Surfing

I was a charter member of the Pacific Beach Surf Club in 1959 and was president in 1961-62. In the summer of 1963 I was asked to join the Windansea Surf Club as a charter member. I had won several paddling contests, so I was on WSC's paddling team with Butch Van Artsdalen, Rusty Miller, Phil Edwards, and Bill Caster. We won all our events in 1963, including the inaugural Malibu Contest and the West Coast Surf Championships at Huntington Beach. (I missed the infamous bus ride to Malibu because I was working. The bus ride was so raucous that the bus driver refused to drive the bus back to S.D.).

WSC went to Hawaii in December 1963 for the World Surfing Championship at Makaha. I made it to the semi-finals where the waves were 20' and breaking from the point. I had never been so scared in my life. The biggest surf that I had been in prior to that was about 8'. It was at this event that Tom Keck took a picture of our team with Duke Kahanamoku at Makaha. It took 9 hours to get from San Francisco to Honolulu on a TWA Stratocruiser 4 engine prop plane. We stayed at the Waianae Church Camp. Going into town and partying at night was probably not what the church had in mind for guests at their camp.

I got married in 1965 to my current wife and have three children and nine grandchildren.

More surf stories

This story was re-told in a book called Parafin Chronicles. Parafin after the wax we used in the 50's and 60's. Basically wax that was used for canning jams and jellies. Certainly a lot cheaper than the custom designer wax that is produced today.

Hawaii

In December 1963, the Windansea Surf Club went to Hawaii
for the World Championships in Makaha on the island of Oahu.
The club took the "senior" members of the club (18 to 30 years
old) and junior members (under 18). I was 19 at the time and
one of the youngest seniors. A lot of the junior members were
surfers who I surfed with both in Pacific Beach and La Jolla.
So I knew them pretty well. I usually was their chauffeur since
they didn't drive. None of us had been to Hawaii before, so
we wanted to check out other parts of the island, especially the
North Shore. The North Shore was featured in every surfing
movie. Surf spots like Pipeline, Sunset Beach, and Waimea
Bay. Waimea Bay is known for its huge and pounding waves –
25 foot plus at times.

The day we drove to the North Shore I was one of maybe
two senior members and about 6 or so juniors. The Club had
rented a passenger van so we were able to get our surfboards in
it. The surf on the North Shore was reported to be small, so I
didn't take my board on the trip. When we got to Waimea Bay,
there was no surf at all. Maybe some small swells rolling over
the inside reefs. One of the juniors, his name was Larry, asked
me if he could paddle out – just to say that he had paddled out
at Waimea Bay and impress his friends back home. Since there
was no surf, I allowed him to go out. When the surf is big it
breaks about 1/3 mile off shore. When Larry was about half the
way out, I suddenly realized that him going out alone wasn't a
good idea. I asked some the other juniors if they would let me
use their board, but they didn't want to risk getting their boards
damaged. I finally persuaded one of them and paddled out after
Larry. I met him outside and told him we should paddle in

because you never know when a rogue wave could come along and knock you off your board (leashes weren't used at that time) and you could drown. Reluctantly he paddled in and I breathed a sigh of relief thinking that he could have been hurt. In the book the story was embellished to say that the surf was 15 feet and I saved Larry's life from a huge wave. I saw the author later on and told him of his exaggeration. He just said – It was a better story with the surf bigger. I saw Larry a few years back at Windansea's 50th anniversary. He was still saying that I saved his life. I think he was more scared at the time than he would admit.

Africa

I am able to claim that I have surfed in three oceans – the Pacific, the Atlantic and the Indian. I surfed the Indian Ocean in June 2005, when my wife and I visited my son and his family who were living in Nairobi, Kenya, serving as missionaries. Although Nairobi is six hours by car to Mombasa on the Indian Ocean, my son had brought his 9'0 surfboard with him. During our visit he had planned some excursions for us, including a safari (of course), a hike on Mt. Kenya, the second tallest peak in Africa, and a trip to Milindi on the east coast. The safari to the Masai Mara was rained out and the hike to Mt. Kenya was cut short about halfway up the mountain because of a bug I picked up at the primitive home of a native Kenyan family my son had befriended. That left the trip to Milindi as an opportunity for a relaxing time and to experience the culture of coastal Kenya – and maybe a chance to get some waves.

The total trip time to the resort at Milindi was about eight hours. My wife said "no way" to riding in a Mitsubishi SUV with seven other people plus luggage and a board on top. She opted to fly to the resort with my daughter-in-law, a two hour flight, while my son, his four kids and I drove the two lane main highway to the coast. The route skirts the northern edge of the Serengeti Game Preserve with Mt. Kilimanjaro looming in the southern sky.

About 30 miles out of Nairobi we encountered the Kenyan version of "road-kill." A giraffe was lying in the middle of the road, having been hit by one of the multitude of trucks hauling freight between Kenya's capital and Mombasa. As we crept past the downed giraffe, it suddenly struggled to its feet and staggered off, revealing a large swath of road rash but still alive. The rest of the trip to Milindi was relatively uneventful considering that the last two hours was traveled primarily on dirt roads.

We arrived at the all-inclusive Turtle Bay Resort, just south of Milindi, tired but unscathed. Of course, we had to endure the verbal jabs from the women as to why we were so tired and dirty and the incredulous question of "what took us so long?" We finally recovered and relaxed in the pool and spa. Then there was dinner at the restaurant where the kids relished the all-you-can-eat buffet.

The next day we broke out the surfboard and caught some small messy wind waves in the afternoon in the 85° water. Hardly the best waves I've ever ridden, but I was surfing in Africa in the Indian Ocean. My son was attending a "Men's Retreat" put on by his church, so we spent the next two days snorkeling, windsurfing and hanging out at the beach and pool.

The third day my son and I went looking for surf. We set out shortly after dawn and headed north about 5 miles to the heart of Milindi where we had been told we might find waves in the bay fronting the town. We cruised through town, receiving curious looks from the Milindeans at the rare sight of a surfboard strapped to the top of a car. We stopped near a small fishing pier to check the bay and "yes!!" we could see some waves about a mile up the beach. We traveled to a likely pathway to the beach and maneuvered our way along the sandy road and discovered "surf."

At 7:00 am we were the "dawn patrol" but we weren't really worried about crowded waves or "locals." What we saw were fairly well shaped 3-4' beachbreak waves with a slight offshore wind and no one out. It's always a little "sketchy" surfing an unknown break with no one else out. You wonder about the condition of the water, what the bottom and the line up is like, how the waves will break, and, of course, what other creatures may be inhabiting the same water that you're splashing around in. We only had one board and a pair of bodysurfing fins between us. My son got first pick to ride the board and I got to be the "chum" in the water bodysurfing. We both got some clean waves body and board surfing and we came out of the water with all of our limbs intact and not dripping blood. It was a fun surf session and we scored some unexpectedly good waves.

The next day we were facing the arduous eight hour trip back to Nairobi, but it was bearable because everyone enjoyed their time at the resort, and as a bonus my son and I got some good waves. My wife and daughter-in-law took the easy way out and flew home, while the rest of us set out to tackle the rugged pot-holed Kenyan highway to Nairobi.

It was "smooth sailing" until about 3-1/2 hours into the drive when we encountered a log-jam of trucks blocking the road for miles on end. Apparently, bandits had robbed one of the truckers earlier in the morning, so the rest of the truckers decided to band together to protest the lack of police security. Finding out that we weren't going to get past the impact area until the next day, we back-tracked to find an alternate route.

Mission organizations provide information to their people to prepare them for evasive actions when lives are in jeopardy. My son had been given maps showing various escape routes. We pulled out the maps and plotted a route around the plugged travel artery. The alternate route turned out to be the safari we had missed out on previously. The dirt single-lane road was a circuitous trip through the Serengeti Game Preserve. We encountered a myriad of wildlife, including zebras, gazelles, and a bull elephant about 50 feet from the road.

Four hours later, with the sun setting over the cloud-shrouded Mt. Kilimanjaro, we ended our Serengeti adventure and pulled back onto the highway. Fortunately, we entered the road just ahead of the miles of cars, buses and trucks packing the two-lane vehicular lifeline between Kenya's two main cities. Eleven hours after we began, with the lights of Nairobi in sight, we were nearing the end of our trek. We all had dreams of a meal, a shower to wash off several layers of dirt, and a bed to ease our achy muscles. A flat tire ended those dreams, and the tire change bordered on a nightmare. Par for the trip home so far. We finally arrived at my son's house some 12 hours after the journey began, to the tongue-in-cheek greetings from the well-rested and refreshed women saying, "what took you so long?" It was one of those moments when sarcasm is marginally endured.

All in all, it was still a good trip to the coast. Adventure, agony, fun, frustration, and a chance to tell an adventurous surf story to someone that would start with: "You should have seen the surf we got in Africa."

Triathlons

I also did triathlons for about 13 years from about 1982 to 1995. At one time I was ranked number nine in my age group for two years in a row. I did the Hawaii Ironman Race in 1990, but I didn't have a good time of it. I ended up in the hospital with severe magnesium depletion and "hypo-natremia," which is basically abnormally low salt content in your body

Ironman Triathlon

I participated in the Hawaii Ironman Triathlon in 1990. I say participated because I wasn't competitive in the race and I was just barely able to finish. The distance of a full Ironman race is 2.4 mile swim, 112 mile bike ride, and a marathon, 26.2 miles. Being in Hawaii, the weather is very humid and warm. Often there are strong trade winds blowing. So a person considering doing the race doesn't just wake up one morning a month before the race and decide that they are going to enter. By 1990 I had been doing triathlons for about 8 years. In 1989 I had done an Ironman equivalent race in Lake Tahoe and finished 2nd in my age group. A couple of months later, I did a Half Ironman in Arizona and won my age group. So by 1990 I felt pretty confident that I could complete the race in Hawaii.

The race is held in October of every year on the night of a full moon so racers can see when they are running at night. But you can't just enter the race and be admitted. A person has to qualify in another triathlon to be selected to participate. I did a qualifying race in Arizona in May and missed the cut-off for qualification. I came in 2nd instead of 1st. So I had to compete in a race in Texas in September in hopes of qualifying. I finished 2nd there too, but in this race the top three received Ironman entries.

I wanted to make sure that I was fully prepared to do all the distances in the Hawaii race. But what I did was over-train and went into the race tired from excessive training.

The race started at 7:00 am at the Kailua-Kona Pier. The 2.4-mile swim went well and I finished in about 1 hour 10 min. The first half of the 112-mile bike leg is relatively easy. The temperature and humidity is relatively low. The only difficult part is riding about 10 miles up a long grade to the town of Hawi for the turn around. There are aid stations about every 5 miles on the bike leg and one in Hawi. Because a racer has to make sure they are hydrated, what goes in has to come out. The phrase known in the Ironman is the "pee at Hawi." You actually pee in your bike shorts while you are pedaling back down the hill. You pour water over your legs so you don't smell like urine.

The bike ride back to Kona is the brutal part of the race. You have to ride through the lava fields with the black pavement and the black lava radiating the heat back on each racer. In 1990 it was hotter and windier than usual. The elite and younger racers are able to get through this section earlier and avoid the heat and wind. The older and not quite so fit (I was 45 at the time) get beat up.

I finally finished the bike leg about 2:30 pm. Time for a marathon in the heat and humidity of a Hawaiian afternoon. Because I had over-trained, I wasn't able to digest food and water well. My run consisted to making it from porta-potty to porta-potty. I tried to drink Gatorade, but it upset my stomach. So

I just drank water. The sun went down and I still had about 10 miles to run. I finished at about 9:00 pm after 14 hours of racing. With about ¼ of a mile to go, an older woman ran past me to the finish line. I found out later that she was a 60 year old nun. After the race, I stumble to the aid tent. My feet were swollen and had blisters on the bottom. The swelling was from a condition called hypo-natremia – lack of salt/electrolytes in your body. Drinking water keeps fluids in the body, but causes swelling because the water will pool in your extremities. Some people get swelling in their brain.

I was transported to the hospital where I was given an IV of fluids with a high content of magnesium. My magnesium levels had plummeted, similar to a highly intoxicated person who gets the DT's. I woke up the next morning and felt fine after my electrolyte replenishment.

I took a year off from doing triathlons after that. The training has a big effect on family time. I owed that next year to my wife, who had endured a year of my Ironman training (6 to 8 hours a day) and then the race that put me in the hospital.

I raced triathlons a few time from 1993 to 1995. I was promoted to an administrative job in the Fire Department effective January 1996. In December of 1995 I was hit by a car while I was riding my bike. Nothing was broken except for my bike. I was just bruised and cut up. I did register a 9.5 for my back flip through the air from being hit from behind. I failed to get a 10 because the car assisted my back-flip.

Fire Department

I started with the San Diego Fire Department in 1967. The second week on probation, I became sick with the chicken pox.

I probably came close to being fired, but I was able to make up all my tests and drills. I took my probation on a 1947 fire engine. When I retired, I was in charge of the first helicopter program for San Diego City.

As a firefighter, I was once searching and crawling through a house that was on fire. It was very smoky and hot and my vision was even further obscured from the breathing apparatus that I was wearing. As I crawled along I ran into a skeleton, and at first I thought "this guy is burned really bad." But it was only a biology lab skeleton. The firemen outside could hear me screaming.

At a fire where someone did die (from smoke inhalation), I cut my hand on a broken window. I was taken to the hospital and was put in the ER in a bed next to the bed where the corpse was lying – really bright red from carbon monoxide inhalation. I imagined him sitting up and yelling one last time – Yikes!!!

I was a tillerman on a "hook and ladder" truck. If you weren't buckled into the seat, you could get thrown out going around a curve or going down a hill with bumps (Like riding a roller coaster in the back seat). Engineers (drivers) who were new to the truck were the scariest.

As an engineer (driver), I was stationed at the Airport crash and rescue station and drove the big airport fire trucks. I didn't respond to any major incidents at the Airport, and it was the most boring station I ever had. I was also on the City's Rescue Squad. We responded to numerous traffic accidents where we cut and pried people out of vehicles.

I later moved to a station near UCSD. We responded to a roll-over traffic accident on I-805 after midnight one night. It was a van with a single passenger that was upside down. The driver had her foot caught in between the brake pedal and the dash board. Using my skills from the Rescue Unit, I looked into the van to determine how to free her foot and discovered that her leg had a compound fracture and was almost severed. I climbed inside the van, freed her foot, and held her leg together while she was removed out the back of the van. My captain, who I had worked with before and was a friend of mine, told me (joking of course) that I was trying to look up her dress. Very funny – not.

As a captain I served in fire operations and the Fire Prevention Bureau. I once inspected Jerome's Furniture Warehouse in downtown San Diego. Jerry Jerome was resisting my notice to clean up his furniture refinishing area – that is until there was a fire in the same area about a week after I had done the inspection. He called me and said he would do whatever was needed to bring the finishing area into compliance.

While in Fire Ops, we went to a fire at a large older hotel in downtown San Diego. One crew went up the rear fire escape to attack the fire. My crew went in from the front and we helped people escape. I met the attack crew at the fire escape on the floor below the room that was on fire. But the crew decided to connect the hose right outside the fire floor – against all training. The attack crew got the hose right up to the fire and the door at the fire escape shut over the hose – no water!!! The captain was yelling in a shrill and panicked voice "Help, it's hot!!!" Of course it was hot – there wasn't any water flowing. We finally got the hose untangled and put out the fire. But he never lived down: "Help it's hot!!!" Firemen are merciless if you make a mistake.

Education

I was able to complete my bachelor's degree in Public Administration in 1981 by going to college part time on and off in the 19 years after I finished high school. I also earned a certificate in Fire Administration. I earned an AA degree in Fire Science in 1972.

I was promoted to Battalion Chief in 1983 and was put in charge of developing a hazardous materials inspection program for the City. It was implemented in 1985. One of the first businesses to be inspected was my uncle's auto paint supply store. He called me and said it was going to cost him $30,000 to $40,000 to fix everything. "Could I do something about it" he asked? I said no I can't, and recused myself from being directly in charge of any decision regarding his business. He later thanked me for making him do the work.

I was on the Normal Heights brush fire that burned down 60 homes in June 1985. The flames were about 30 feet high over the tops of the homes along the canyon. Fire brands were dropping on roofs 2 blocks away from the fire. The team I was with was literally surrounded by fire.

After serving in Fire Prevention, I was assigned to Fire Ops in the beach area – Pt. Loma, Ocean Beach, Pacific Beach and La Jolla. It was like the fox guarding the henhouse. I was back to my old stomping grounds from where I grew up surfing. Of course I had to drive by the beach a lot to make sure there were no fires burning there.

I was promoted to Deputy Chief (two steps down from Fire Chief) in 1996 and put in charge of Fire Ops for the 1996 Republican National Convention at the downtown Convention Center. During the course of the RNC, the City incurred some personnel costs for a particular event. The FBI rep told me I should just bill the Secret Service for the costs. Little did I know at the time that there was a rivalry that wasn't always friendly between the FBI and the SS. I sent the SS a $10,000 bill and got a nasty phone call from the Agent in Charge. I figured out that the FBI rep set me up for that one. I was eventually put in charge of Fire Ops for the whole City. My pager was going off day and night. Putting in an eight hour day, after a night out at a fire, was rough.

My last job on the Fire Department was developing and putting in to service the first helicopter program for the City. We didn't have sufficient funding, so we tried to get corporate sponsorship to fill the funding gap. We were able to secure the majority of the funding from the County of San Diego. The Mayor and one of the County Supervisors ran against each other in the previous mayor's race. The Supervisor lost, so he was more than happy to provide some funding to help the City as a jab to the Mayor. I had to do a lot of political dancing while working between the Supervisor and the Mayor. The Police had helicopters for police work, but they weren't suitable for fire ops. The Mayor knew he was stuck, but wanted to hear from me during the Council hearing why there was a need for "two air forces in the City." Donna Frye, Skip Frye's wife, was a Councilperson at the time. I knew her pretty well from my ties with Skip. I could see her smirk as I was being grilled by the Mayor. Despite the Mayor's objections, the helicopter program was funded for a 3-month pilot program in August of 2002.

The helicopter responded to two large brush fires in the first two days of service. At the second fire, the Fire Chief wanted to play a prank on me. He wrote my name on a road flare and gave it to a police officer – implying that maybe I had started the fire to get the new helicopter some work and media attention. The police officer went along with the gag by handing me the flare and telling me the Fire Chief want to know what this flare with my name on it was all about!!! I had been gooned again.

I retired from the Fire Department in November 2002, after 35 years and almost not making it past the first two weeks. It was ironic that I took my probation on a 1940's vintage fire engine and I left on a helicopter.

Since my retirement, I have been on the Board of Directors of the California Surf Museum and the HOA where I live. At the Surf Museum I was a project manager for the new facility on Pier View Way.

The Cardiff Coffee Club is a weekly enjoyment – Swapping stories from the La Jolla and South Bay crews, and of course listening to some of Woody's new jokes.

- six -

Tommy Carroll

It was November 9th, 1955, and it was cold. I was flying my final check ride when Speck Winchester of Pan American World Airways walked in to my flight school. He was out scouting for pilots and there I was up in the air (literally) and missing all the interviews! Luckily one of my classmates, Joe Bello, must have said a few good words about me to Speck and that I would be interested in flying for Pan Am. Speck gave Joe his card to give to me, and asked that I should give him a call. Speck apparently checked my record and saw that I had the necessary licenses before he flew back to the company headquarters in San Francisco, because when I called him the next day, he said "I'll hire you. All you have to do is pass the physical. When can you be here?" "Tomorrow!" I said – I knew about pilot seniority!

Five days later on November 14, 1955, I started ground school and flight training on the Boeing 377, 4-engine Stratocruiser. Later I got navigation training to obtain a FAA Navigator License.

On February 10, 1956, I had my first flight from San Francisco to Honolulu. In those days there were no modern

Inertial Guidance Systems or GPS. Pan Am crossed the oceans, navigating by the stars, so a night flight took 9 hours and 30 minutes for the crossing in the Stratocruiser. Of course I had a another navigator giving me supervised navigation training. We landed well after midnight and the trade winds had died down to a gentle breeze. You could smell the Plumeria and the air was soft and fragrant. When a limo picked us up and took us to the Moana Hotel right on world famous Waikiki beach, it felt pretty grand!

For a beach boy who had grown up in La Jolla, I was right at home. In those days, the Outrigger Club was between the Royal Hawaiian Hotel and the Moana Hotel. The Outrigger Club liked Pan Am, as we were the first airline to fly to Hawaii from the mainland. PAA started that service in November of 1935, and a few months later we crossed the Pacific all the way to China in a Martin 130. This famous flying boat was called the "China Clipper," landing in the lagoons of Midway, Wake Island, Guam and Manila.

In those days, Pan Am personnel experienced a special Aloha spirit from the Hawaiians. The Outrigger Club treated the flight crews very well. They gave us a place to store our surf boards and a special rate of $5 per year for full membership for using the club for surfing, volley ball, dining, and use of the bar. For me, the best deal was the surf board. I would take the PAA board out in the morning and spend the day catching the waves. We always had at least a 24-hour layover then.

One of the interesting flights I had was to Saigon on July 27, 1956. By then I was a licensed navigator. We arrived in Saigon after stops in Honolulu, Wake Island and Manila. We were all fascinated by Saigon and avidly toured the city. At that time, it was still French Indochina but the French had been defeated by the Vietnamese and were in the process of pulling out.

Although the city was peaceful, the French had a few machine guns barricaded with sand bags around their barracks. The troops were in white shorts and shirts and appeared not to be too interested in fighting any longer. They were more interested in lunch and drinking some fine French wine.

The Vietnamese had decimated their base in the Battle of Dien Bien Phu by Ho Chi Minh's Viet Minh forces that were 40,000 strong. After that, we no longer laid over in Saigon, but flew down to Singapore and stayed at the old Raffles hotel. I would go with the crew to the bar and enjoy a Singapore Sling, made famous at the Raffles hotel. This was all daylight flying, as we had airway beacon to follow. After a nice layover, we then retraced out route home to San Francisco.

In the late 1950s, on one my frequent flights to Hawaii, I was fortunate to buy Pat Curren's (the big-wave surfer of the day) 1942 Dodge. He was leaving for the Mainland. The price was $35 **AND** including a surfboard rack **AND** a lot of stuff in the back seat, including letters from the girls he dated! I wish I had saved them, as they would be priceless today. So now, with that old Dodge, I had a way to get out into the country away from Waikiki.

My favorite surf spot was Makaha, on the west coast of Oahu. A big Hawaiian, named Buffalo was the life guard. Buzzy Trent also lived out there, and another friend of mine from La Jolla named Junior Knox. I bought a Velzy gun for big waves, which were in abundance at Makaha. Life was good!

In the mid-1960s, life in the Island changed with the Americans involved in the Vietnam War. Pan Am was flying R

& R flights to Honolulu for the troops. With that, there was a definite change on the island of Oahu.

Pan Am ushered in the Jet Age in 1959. Tourists were flocking into the Island and more hotels were being built. Henry Kaiser built the Hawaiian Village and Chang built the Ilikai. I remember the condos at the Ilikai were selling for $9,900. I should have bought one.

By 1969 I was a co-pilot on the B 707, hoping to make Captain. When that did not happen, I took a leave of absence from PAA and flew down to New Zealand with my girlfriend, Jean, who later became my wife. Jean was a beautiful redhead whom I met in 1967 when she was a stewardess with PAA. Jean shared my sailing dreams and there, in New Zealand, we began the long and arduous, but satisfying task of building our own sailing yacht. Jean turned out to be an incredible sailor, having grown up on an island in San Francisco Bay – that island being Alcatraz! Her dad was a guard there and when Jean went to school, her "bus" was a boat!

When we finally finished building our yacht, the Windrift, we set sail across the South Pacific. Among our ports of call were the Islands of Fiji, Tonga and the Cooks. We stayed almost a year in Tahiti, sailing the nearby islands of Moorea, Huahine, Tahaa and Bora Bora. For four years we explored the Pacific, always looking for new surf spots. Luckily, I had my Carl Ekstrom surfboard with me. Sometimes PAA flight crews on a Tahiti layover would drop by the yacht, and we would take them out to the Bali Hai on Moorea, which is only 7 miles away.

Jean and I had flown a lot of trips to Tahiti. Back then we had 7-day layovers, so the PAA crews would take the ferry over to Moorea and stay at the Bali Hai for their layovers. The Bali

Hai boys treated us very well and we always told our passengers that the only place to stay in Tahiti was the Bali Hai. With PR like this, our Pan American crews made their hotel! Thus, we were very popular with the Bali Hai's owners – Muk, Jay and Kelly!

After four years of cruising the South Pacific, it was time to go back to work. So we sailed back to San Diego, via Honolulu. I went back into training for the B707, after which I got a Captain bid to fly the Inter-German Service out of Berlin Tempelhof. We rented an apartment there for 3 years and I flew the B727 all over Germany and other European cities. By 1980 I got a bid to fly the B747 as Captain, so we left Berlin and I began flying from San Francisco to London, over the pole. I also flew the long-haul, non-stop Pacific flights to Tokyo – no more stops in Honolulu or Wake Island.

Six years later, Pan Am was going broke and sold their Pacific routes to United. I knew it was only a matter of time before PAA would go under, so when United offered me a job flying for them, I took it. United was very good to me. So good, in fact, that they gave me the Boeing 747 400, the latest model aircraft in the world at that time, to fly. I was flying SFO to Hong Kong, non-stop for 13 to 15 hours, and LA to Sydney, non-stop! It was pure luxury for me and my crew. We had a sound proof state-room in the cockpit, plus I had three pilots besides myself to divvy-up the flying hours! I felt that I got paid for sleeping! The salary was good too. However, in March, 1991, all this good life came to an end. I had turned 60 years old and, according to the FAA, I was too old to fly and was forced to retire. My 36 years of flying had now ended, so Jean and I could fly anywhere in the world for free, and we did.

In 1992 We rebuilt the "Windrift" and sailed back to New Zealand via the Marquesas Islands, French Polynesia, Tuamotu Atolls, Tahiti, Fiji and then New Zealand. We planned to sail to Europe, but Jean, being the smart one with the dry wit, said to me: "You know, we could do this a lot cheaper and easier if we went by cruise ship. I would not have to cook, or stand an anchor watch, or do a sail change at 3:00 a.m.!" And, with that, we sold the yacht in New Zealand and began to enjoy the comforts of cruising the world on the Seabourn line of ships.

- seven -

Tommy Dunne

When Tommy sent me his sparse notes on his life story, I only understood his brevity and minimalist approach to sharing that information when he advised me that he and Sharon had just been traveling for 24+ straight hours from Vietnam, returning from a lengthy visit with their son Cory and his family.

Of course that didn't stop Tommy from attending our Tuesday morning meeting at Howard Bugbee's rehab unit, although Tommy was probably so jetlagged that I'm not sure he could remember his own name. Even being able to function at all must have been an old pilot trick.

When asked what he thought of Vietnam, Tommy stated it was a wonderful experience to see how Cory, Lauren, and their grandkids were thriving in such a different environment.

Let's get on with the story of Tommy's life, shall we?

Tommy was born in November 1939 in Denver, Colorado. His family moved to Hermosa Beach in December 1939.

No messing around with the Dunne family! They got to the

sweet spot, a.k.a. Hermosa Beach, when Tommy had only just turned one month old!

Tommy attended the usual public schools in the South Bay. He was a Cub Scout, played Little League baseball, and Pop Warner football for the Hermosa Beach Little Ringers.

Upon entering junior high at Pier Avenue and hanging out at the Manhattan Beach pier watching Velzy, Beth Morgan, John McFarlane, and the other "old guys," Tommy got the surf bug.

Tommy's first surfboard was shaped by Greg Noll in Greg's back yard.

Tom attended Mira Costa High School, where he first got together with Skip Stratton.

Tommy surfed a lot. He related that high school at Mira Costa was always a challenge for him because he had to choose between a good swell or the dreary classroom. Seems like that was another common denominator shared by the members of our gang, isn't that right Woody?

On one occasion, he ditched the first two periods of school and borrowed Phil Harmon's car to go to the Redondo Breakwater.

Mira Costa had a closed campus policy and every once in a while the cops patrolled the parking lot. Unfortunately, Tommy picked the "while" to return to the school parking lot and was busted in his wetsuit!

Mrs. Harmon, Phil's mother, had no knowledge of anybody using the car. Therefore the police escorted Tommy directly to the slammer in his black rubber wetsuit.

Tommy's take on the whole episode was this:

"When I surfed in high school, I got detention. Now
the kids receive sports letters!"

And then there was Carl Fisher. Carl was the Boy's Vice Principal
at Mira Costa and really a great guy. Every time the boys would
show up early in the morning at the Redondo Breakwater, Carl
would be waiting. "Mister Fisher, how did you know?" "North
swell," he said. "Get to class."

Tommy said they had forgotten that Carl ran on the beach
every day. He also reports that Carl remained a family friend and
was invited to Tom and Sharon's wedding.

As I've been looking at Tommy's life story, I noticed that there
seems to be a common syndrome that has run rampant through
many of our members. That syndrome can best be described as:
"Oh what the hell, since I'm bored, let's try something new and
totally different (at the drop of a hat!)."

Worked for Tommy.

After graduating from high school, Tommy enrolled at El
Camino College in Torrance. However, his college matriculation
lasted only until someone said to him: "Wanna go to Hawaii
and surf for a while?"

When you're a member of our venerated gang, there can
be only one answer to that question. "When do we leave for
Hawaii?"

Tom did want to go surfing in Hawaii, and in 1958 did just

that for a year. He spent the summer on a houseboat in the Ala Moana yacht harbor, and the winter on the North Shore, living in a Quonset hut in Haleiwa.

Then he got serious about his education and actually managed to go to college for a full year. Of course that only lasted until someone came up to Tommy and inquired: "Wanna take a trip around the country?"

Once again, Tommy's DNA required him to answer in the affirmative.

That led to a six-month trip around the country, including a trip to Cuba where Tommy, in his words, "watched Castro take over."

That's all Tommy said in his notes. By now I'm sure you recognize the fact that your intrepid reporter (that would be me) isn't about to let that kind of casual bombshell go unnoticed.

When pressed, Tommy told the following story.

He couldn't remember whether was 1958 or 1959. However, since his year of surfing in Hawaii occurred in 1958, we have to assume it was 1959.

Based upon my checking the history of Castro's takeover of Cuba, in fact it may have been late 1958.

When Tommy and his two buddies reached Key West, they saw an ad for Cubana Airlines. It offered a round-trip ticket to Cuba with a visa for only $29. Tommy and his two buddies couldn't pass up that kind of deal!

When they reached Cuba, they hooked up with a friend

of a friend and decided to drive out of Havana for a week of camping at a beach about 80 miles outside of the city, in Puerto Escondido.

On the way to their destination, they came across a roadblock manned by well-dressed and well-equipped soldiers in neat khaki uniforms. In Tom's words, they were "(Dictator) Baptista's boys."

On the way back to Havana after spending the week camping on the beach, Tommy and his friends received their first indication that a revolutionary war in Cuba was taking place at that very moment!

When they came upon the same roadblock again, this time it was manned by bearded soldiers in olive green fatigues, "Castro's boys." While they had been surfing the days away, Castro had managed to overthrow the Batista government.

Checking the historical records, this would've been during the first few days of 1959.

When I asked Tommy if he and his friends were in any danger following the revolutionary coup, he answered in the negative because at that time, Castro and his people thought very highly of the United States. Some of the revolutionaries they talked with even said that they had been assisted in their training and instruction concerning weapons handling by some of the Marines at Guantánamo.

Of course the subsequent Bay of Pigs changed all of that.

Tommy got back to the beach just in time for the spring semester at El Camino college. Time to really bear down on his education. Next came summer school.

Tommy's next move was in keeping with his gypsy lifestyle. As the following semester started, he went to a Warren Miller ski movie. Tommy had always wanted to learn how to ski, and what better way to learn than to go someplace where you can ski every day.

Thus began Tom's love affair with Aspen. He spent a year in Aspen waiting on tables at night and skiing his brains out every day.

The next year Tommy, almost 21, got the educational itch again. Time to get serious. He knew how to surf and ski, had a fake ID to get past Howard in the Poop Deck, and lived in a bitch'n party house in Hermosa Beach.

As fate would have it, one night at a party at his house, Tony Arce walked in with this petite, tanned, beach girl Tommy had never seen before.

It just so happened that she had grown up in Hermosa Beach, just 10 blocks from Tommy's family home. She had gone to Catholic schools and was attending San Jose State.

Tommy claims that he knew that night that Sharon was going to be the one who he wanted to be with for the rest of his life. She used her sister's ID (sorry to spring this on you Howard!), and their first date was at the Poop Deck.

However, after one more year of education, Tommy successfully overcame the educational seduction once again with great elan. "Boring!!" Tommy was hit by the travel bug again, and he decided he had time for one last fling before settling down.

To suggest that Tommy was rather rootless in his youth might be an overly broad characterization. However, his next move certainly leaned heavily in that direction.

What to do next? That's easy. In 1961 someone said to Tommy:

"Wanna go to Europe?"

For an ordinary person that might be a tough question to deal with. However, as the reader may have noted, there's a pattern developing here when it comes to Tommy's responses to his friends' "suggestions."

Mister round heels personified!! Of course Tommy thought it was a capital idea to take off and go to Europe. What did you expect?

The way it developed was this. One night at the Poop Deck, he and Jerry Shoemaker figured if they sold their cars, they could afford to go to Europe. Tommy discovered a trip on the North German Lloyd Line "Bremen," for only $200, from New York to Bremerhaven, Germany. They saw the ad in the paper for riders wanting to drive to New York.

So Tommy and Jerry took off and went to Europe. They hitchhiked all around Europe and then got jobs during the ski season, working on the ski patrol, in Davos, Switzerland.

At the end of the ski season at Davos, Tommy finally decided, in his early 20s, that maybe it was time to grow up, again in his words, "sort of."

The truth of the matter was that after a couple of months and lots of love letters, he realized that if he didn't get back to Sharon, he might lose her. Without further ado, he got back!

So Tommy returned to Hermosa Beach. Luckily, Sharon had waited for him. They got married on June 23, 1962, at American Martyrs Catholic Church, and then celebrated their marriage at the Pen and Quill in Manhattan Beach.

Sharon taught school in Hermosa Beach until their first son, Kevin, was born in May, 1963.

As a precursor to Tommy's career as a general contractor, Tommy worked is a carpenter during the day and attended Cal State Long Beach in the evenings, on his way to obtaining a BA in Physical Education.

One of his part-time jobs was at Air Research testing John Glenn's spacesuit!!

Tommy then had a short career in pharmaceutical sales and did a little bit of substitute teaching.

In another abrupt career course correction (something that appears to be a common thread running through our gang), Tommy started taking flying lessons.

At the time, the airlines were hiring a few pilots without military experience.

After obtaining the requisite pilot licenses, Tommy worked in various flying jobs to build up sufficient experience (pilot hours) to be able to apply for a slot as a pilot on a commercial airline.

Eventually, after submitting numerous resumes, he was hired by Golden West-Catalina Airlines, flying Twin Otters out of Long Beach.

Flying little twin-engine jet props was not his ultimate goal, so he still had applications out with all the major carriers. When his aircraft was hit while taxiing by a telephone truck at LAX, the media headlines naturally stated "airplane hits truck."

Tommy states it was the other way around. However, as he stated, not good to have his name in the paper as the pilot concerning that incident.

After working with Golden West, he then was hired by United Airlines.

During that period Sharon was teaching school in Palos Verdes and they lived in Hermosa Beach. According to Tom, the surfing was still pretty good.

Unfortunately, after Tommy got settled into being an airline pilot for United flying out of LAX, a couple of surgeries on his left eye due to a previous injury caused by an automobile accident resulted in a medical termination by United.

What to do next? By this point in time Tommy had a family and no longer could respond in the affirmative when a friend came up to him and said: "Tommy, wanna go . . . ?

After flying, Tommy couldn't discover any other job that was interesting to him. Sharon was on maternity leave from Palos Verdes School District at that time, after having son number two, Chris. Given the fact that Sharon could teach school anywhere and they both loved Aspen, Tommy and Sharon decided to head to the mountains.

After arriving in Aspen, upon dining at the Chart House (the first one for the chain) and having dinner comped by his friend and ours, Roy Bream, the manager, he knew they were home.

Son number three, Cory, was born the year they arrived, so the family was complete. When Cory was three, Sharon was hired by the Aspen School District.

Since there was a 12-year difference between the oldest and youngest boy in the Dunne family, folks wanted to know if the last one (Cory) was "an accident." Tommy's answer to them was, "No, the first two were."

According to Tommy, moving to Aspen in 1974 was terrific! The town had not yet been ranked as a world-class resort. It was just a great little mountain town with a population of about 8,000. At that time, you couldn't walk down the street without running into a friend.

Tommy spent 25 years in Aspen working for the Aspen Ski Company.

That employment almost came to a quick end when the Director of the Ski School asked Tommy if he would drive down to Denver in a company truck to pick up a load of new ski school uniforms that had just arrived from Italy.

After picking up the uniforms, Tommy took advantage of the nearness of Applejack Liquors (super discount store) and stopped to shop. When coming out of the store, Tommy noticed, to his horror, that the truck was gone. A kindly lady then tapped him on the shoulder and asked if the truck with the Aspen skiing logo on it, on the other side of the parking lot, was his? Apparently the load on the truck was too much for the parking brake to hold.

Tommy also built upon his carpentry skills by becoming a general contractor and building homes in the Aspen area. In addition, he obtained his real estate license and sold property in and around Aspen.

Tommy relates that Aspen real estate prices have increased on a logarithmic basis. He offered an example. In 1974, he built his first house on 5 acres of land at the Buttermilk ski area for $70,000. That house sold last year for $3.9 million. Unfortunately, Tommy had previously sold the house in 1978 for $385,000!

He and Sharon purchased 38 acres of land, built a home and turned it into a small ranchette, complete with four quarter horses. Tommy: "Ride'n and rope'n . . . yee haw!'

During their stay in the mountains, Tommy skied in the winter, sailed at the Rudi Reservoir (home of the Aspen Yacht Club), and enjoyed mountain biking, hiking, golfing, and hanging around the ranch with the family and horses.

According to Tommy, living in Aspen was wonderful and it was a great town for the kids to grow up, but California was calling him and Sharon back. By then the kids had finished college, Kevin at UCSB, and Chris and Cory at the University of Colorado, Boulder. In addition, Kevin had moved back to California and Tommy's first grandson had arrived in Hermosa Beach.

So, in 1997, they decided that it was time to move back to the beach.

When they were considering the move from Aspen and into retirement, Hermosa Beach had become, at least in their estimation, overcrowded.

Sharon's sister, Sheila, and her family, had moved to Leucadia years before where Tommy had been a frequent visitor. They liked the area.

They scouted around and found a lot at Morgan Run, where Tommy built their present home on the golf course. They became members of the Morgan Run Club and Resort. They have also had an opportunity to enjoy tennis, golf, and hiking.

Tommy and Sharon still travel a lot, having just returned from Vietnam where their son Cory works for the US Department of Homeland Security. They have a small condo in Aspen and spend time there, both in the summer and winter.

Having an opportunity to get back to his lifelong love for surfing, Tommy's longtime friend, Greg Hoberg, another Hermosa Beach transplant and Pipes surf regular, introduced him to the Pipes' crew and that became his home break.

So how did Tommy hook up with the Tuesday Morning Gang?
Tommy puts it this way:

"One evening while strolling along 101 in Encinitas, I saw this bitch'n '57 Chevy Bel Air with Skip sitting on the curb next to it. I hadn't seen much of Skip after we both graduated from high school. Skip told me about Tuesday mornings, and here I am. I had no idea that I would run into other old HB guys like Pat, Roy, and

Bobby. The ultimate surprise (and shock) happened when Pat asked, "Do you know Howard Bugbee?"

Tommy's immediate concern was that he was afraid Howard would remember all those times when Howard had busted Tommy trying to get into the Poop Deck with his fake ID!

Tommy's assessment of retirement is similar to that shared by the rest of our gang. Retirement is good!

He still enjoys golf and surfing (although not so much surfing any more), and working around the house, but not in the garden! He skis every winter and he and Sharon are free to travel when and where they choose. Tommy states that just kicking back with a good book is not a bad option either.

Lastly, Tommy states that "One of the perks of retirement is being able to attend the Tuesday morning 'meeting' with my buds at Seaside Market."

- eight -

Jack "Woody" Ekstrom

[This was originally written about Woody in a history of Leucadia and specifically, "Neptune Avenue, Avenue of the Stars."
I wrote a similar piece about Bobby Beathard.]

Another iconic sports celebrity who lives on our famous beach street is Woody Ekstrom, who is a longtime friend of mine.

In spite of our friendship, I will try to be objective in discussing his life and accomplishments. However, if in doing so I become overly effusive in telling his story, please bear with me. You will just have to chalk it up to the fact that I feel so strongly about this wonderful gentlemen and what he has achieved during his life.

Woody Ekstrom was born in 1927 in Illinois. His dad was a Swedish immigrant.

Woody's family moved to San Diego in 1930.

Woody showed me a picture taken in 1937, when he was 10, all dressed up in his marching band uniform. He played clarinet in that band for some years. After they moved to La Jolla, he had to take the trolley downtown to attend band sessions.

There were about 150 kids in the junior band and another

150 in the senior marching band. Our own Richard Clark, "Clarkie," was a member of the senior marching band. They practiced by marching along Laurel Avenue, in downtown San Diego, on Saturday mornings.

One interesting tidbit. Woody's not sure about the spelling, but the band was known as the Bohman Brothers Boys Band. Nothing unusual about that, except they were named after a mortuary. The mortuary was the sponsor for their band!

In 1940, Woody's family relocated to the Windansea area of La Jolla.

From the time when Woody was a little tyke, he was drawn to the ocean. His first surfing efforts involved riding the whitewater at La Jolla Shores on his mom's ironing board.

At age 12, in 1942, Woody purchased a 13-foot paddleboard for 25 cents.

The next year, 1943, he upgraded to a balsa redwood board which he purchased for $7.50. It was fortunate that the vendor didn't calculate the sales price by the pound. The reason was that the board weighed 72 pounds!

Keep in mind that the person who was hauling this huge surfboard around was a teenager at the time. Not only that, but Woody certainly wasn't the biggest kid on the block.

When an interviewer inquired many years later about Woody's battle scars, emanating from his surfing heroics, Woody did admit that all of his life his right shoulder had been "kind of droopy" from hauling those huge boards around when he was a youngster.

From the time that he first started surfing, Woody had older buddies who he surfed with. However, by 1943 most of his older surfing buddies had gone off to fight in the War.

Not to be deterred, Woody spent considerable time in the summer of 1943 surfing at San Onofre. While there, he became quite familiar with Trestles, one of the foremost surfing spots in all of California.

When the war ended in 1945, his close surfing buddies, as well as most of the members of the Southern California surfing community, were able to return home. They decided to have a reunion in the form of a beach luau in 1946.

As reported by Woody:

"There were about 800 of us there. Guys came from all up and down the coast. The event was not publicized in any way. Everyone learned about it by word-of-mouth. All of us surfers knew each other, and we'd tell who needed to know."

As a matter of fact, Woody claimed that back in those days, even if you didn't recognize an automobile, you could identify the driver by taking a look at the surfboard that was on top of their car.

Woody served in the Army from 1952 to 1954.

He went through boot camp in San Luis Obispo, training to serve in the signal Corps. However, when he shipped out to Germany, where he spent the remainder of his enlistment, he was reassigned to a 90-mm AAA battery.

Woody claims the AAA battery wasn't of much value. The reason was that they couldn't hope to engage the jets that were coming into the Russian military service.

While Woody was serving in Germany, he managed to get up to Sweden and visit with his grandfather.

Because of Woody's lifelong love for music, he also took leave in Paris and attended a concert by Lena Horn, performing in the Moulin Rouge. He also had an opportunity to attend a concert given by Oscar Peterson, accompanying Ella Fitzgerald.

As the members of our group have learned to their astonishment, as witnesses to Woody's constant Jazz travelogue, including jazz trips to Sun Valley for festivals, Woody's love of jazz has been a constant throughout his life.

Some of us are old enough – as a matter of fact I think all of us are old enough!! – to join Woody in his love of records by Artie Shaw, Benny Goodman, and Harry James.

Woody was one of the pioneer surfers in San Diego County. There have been numerous articles written about his surfing exploits. The articles that delve into the history of San Diego County surfing will normally have coverage of some of our Woody's surfing adventures, along with stories about other San Diego County surfing legends.

I would like to share with you one of my favorite Woody surfing stories.

In February, 1947, Woody was out surfing in the La Jolla Cove when the waves purportedly were running 30 to 35 feet high. As someone who has spent quite a bit of time in and around our local oceans over the last 46 years, I can attest to the fact that I have never seen waves anywhere close to that North Shore, Hawaii, magnitude along our beaches.

In any event, on this particular occasion, Woody might've been attempting to operate a cut above his surfing pay grade.

Once Woody had finally struggled out beyond the surfline, the surf was so huge that there was a lifeguard on the beach who was shouting instructions to Woody in an effort to get him safely back to the beach. I can only surmise that the waves were so big that the lifeguard wasn't about to risk his own life by trying to go out and assist Woody if he got in trouble.

As reported by friends on the beach, Woody had the misfortune of having about a 3-½ story wall of water smash down on him and his surfboard. His friends watched the entire humongous liquid train wreck in absolute horror.

As related by Woody, he spent much more time in this industrial-sized whitewater washing machine than was in the best interest of his health.

Frankly, he admitted that he didn't think he was going to make it. At the time he was caught in what was referred to as the "Hole," which is situated adjacent to the La Jolla Cove towards the La Jolla Beach and Tennis Club

Later, when asked by the lifeguard what he was thinking at the critical point under that wave, when he was anticipating an abrupt encounter with the Grim Reaper, his response was a classic Woodyism.

He stated: "My last thoughts were, well I guess I'm going to die a virgin!"

His friends on the beach were thinking that he was a goner for sure. In coming to that conclusion, while Woody was caught up in that chaotic liquid maelstrom, they were so serious about Woody's premature passing that one of their members ran to a phone to call Woody's nearby home. On the phone, he breathlessly advised Woody's mom of Woody's terrible surfing accident.

When he delivered the news, the messenger was so traumatized that Woody's mom later told Woody that she thought he was dead.

Luckily for all of us, to paraphrase Mark Twain's famous quip, reports of Woody's premature demise were extremely exaggerated.

———

The way Woody tells the story, after being mercilessly tossed around by the wave for what seemed like forever, he finally touched bottom.

Once he got his feet down he realized that he could stand up.

The La Jolla Cove is not a good spot to get trapped on the beach by waves that are smashing up against the cliffs. But Woody caught a break. That may be the reason that he still around for all of us to enjoy today.

When he finally was able to stand, he was adjacent to the bluff face. He noted that nearby there were steps that had been cut into the bluff by fishermen. Fortunately, much to the amazement of his friends and the anxious lifeguard, he was able to scramble up those primitive steps and escape the hard-charging monster waves.

As you might imagine, that was the last time that Woody

had an opportunity to use that particular surfboard. When it finally crashed up on the beach, the surfboard was in multiple pieces.

I just got back after chatting again with Woody about his story. He pointed out that the surfboard that was smashed to pieces was one and the same board that appears behind Woody on Woody's iconic business cards. Woody apparently had this board for many years before its climactic demise on that huge wave day.

This near-death experience occurred when Woody was a mere lad of 17 years. We recently helped Woody celebrate his 89th birthday!

In fact he came out of that chaotic oceanic incident suffering only a couple of scratches.

———

Carl Ekstrom, Woody's little brother, who is also iconic in the surfing industry because of his pioneering efforts in creating such things as asymmetric surfboards, was also a member of the Tuesday Morning Gang when I first joined.

These guys have surfed everywhere. During our conversations, when somebody mentions a closely-held secret surfing spot located in some hidden cove somewhere along the California coast, Woody invariably chimes in and starts relating a hilarious story about his experiences at that particularly surfing spot.

———

While I was Googling Woody, I discovered that he was one of the pioneers at surfing what is apparently a famous surf spot down in Imperial Beach, just off of the Tijuana River Sloughs, at the border of Mexico.

What really fascinated me was that I'd never heard anyone, including Woody, mention the surf at the Tijuana Sloughs. Maybe it was because surfing there is so darned gnarly that few, if any, have ever surfed it . . . of course other than Woody and a select few other crazies.

Surfing legend has it that a fellow by the name of Dempsey Holder discovered the Tijuana Sloughs when he tried body surfing at that location back in 1937. If you want to have some fun, Google his name and read up on one of the consummate Watermen and lifeguards of his time. *[BTW, Dempsey Holder was the father of Sean Holder, the present owner of the Pannikin coffee house.]*

Because Dempsey was apparently standing in the wrong line when God was doling out the emotions of fear and trepidation, not to mention common sense, you will discover that some of his insane surfing escapades are totally over-the-top.

Dempsey first pioneered surfing the Sloughs in 1939, all by his lonesome. What made this such a remarkable feat was the way the surf breaks are configured at the Sloughs.

As I understand it, there are three separate breaks, all dictated by the size of the waves. As the waves get bigger, the breaks migrate in a westerly direction.

For the biggest waves, the third and last outside break is purported to be almost a mile off of the beach!

That distance is totally unheard of for the remainder of San Diego County surfing. For example, even with the biggest outside waves at Swami's, Stone Steps, Beacons, or Grandview, a surfer never has to blast his way more than around 50 yards through the onrushing waves and whitewater to reach the largest outside surf break.

The reason for this is that the Tijuana Sloughs enter the ocean as an ancient alluvial fan set by the Tijuana River. This results in a very shallow beach running out towards the ocean as it progresses westward towards the deeper ocean. There is also a reef running out that causes the huge outside waves to peak and pull in surrounding wave energy.

In any event, when Dempsey Holder was surfing solo so far out that it was probably difficult to see him from the beach, he was doing so in waves that could run up from 20 to 30 feet high.

To emphasize just how ginormous those outside wave sets were, Woody swears that if you shouted when you were in the canyon between those monsters, you actually could hear an echo from your shouting.

You also have to keep in mind that at that time in the late 30's, Mr. Holder was surfing with an absolutely huge surfboard which probably weighed close to 100 pounds.

Before he could ever cover that huge distance in order to get to the outside break, he had to paddle that sucker through all of those humongous onrushing waves, not to mention the towering whitewater closer to shore.

Finally, to use platform diving parlance, the degree of difficulty of this athletic feat scored off the charts because of one simple matter. He was surfing without a leash. Surfing leashes came along much later.

Let's consider this scenario. If Dempsey's board got away from him after he had only ridden one wave, that's assuming that he made it beyond the outside surf line, he was first faced with the Herculean task of swimming approximately a mile back to shore and trying to find his surfboard.

After he had completed that portion of the exercise, all he had to do was deal with the unpleasant prospect of once again trying to blast his way through the huge walls of waves and whitewater over that same mile distance in order to be in a position to try to take another ginormous wave.

In reality, Woody has confirmed that usually if you lost your board and had to swim back the mile to the beach, you were so exhausted that you gave it up for the day.

He also reminded me that back in those days, he and Dempsey were surfing those monsters outside waves before the advent of wetsuits. Woody confirmed that it was damn cold that far out in the ocean.

Just to enhance the experience for this adrenaline junkie, for example, if Dempsey had fallen off his board, gotten hit in the head by that monstrous board and knocked silly, he would have been in serious doo doo. Even in the unlikely probability that somebody on the beach could actually observe him that far away and determine that he was in extremis, they couldn't possibly rescue him.

Furthermore, there were no lifeguards in the immediate area. The nearest lifeguard probably would've taken about a half an hour to reach him. Of course that assumes that the lifeguard could actually make it out to where he was, which would have been problematic at best.

So why am I taking this gigantic divergence from my tale about our Leucadia surfing legend, Woody Ekstrom?

The answer is simple. It's because Dempsey Holder was Woody's kind of guy!

In the 40's, when Dempsey had already become a legend in the surfing world, our buddy Woody, still a teenager, couldn't wait to join Dempsey and his very small merry band of mental retards in taking on those gigantic, Hawaiian-sized (on a really big day over there) walls of water.

When Woody was younger, he had all sorts of fascinating characters who were his surfing buddies. He's continually mentioning a fellow by the name of Cromwell to our group. This gentleman first introduced Woody to Dempsey Holder and the Tijuana Sloughs.

Mr. Cromwell went on to become a well-known ocean-ographer. There is a Cromwell Current named in his honor. Mr. Cromwell actually discovered the ocean current, which I believe runs off the coast of Africa. He was also one of the orig-inal oceanographers able to identify the nearshore bottom char-acteristics that create optimum surfing spots.

Woody had another buddy by the name of Woody Brown. Apparently Mr. Brown fell into a rather nice arrangement when he married an extremely wealthy young lady. This marriage permitted Mr. Brown to have the luxury to pursue endeavors that the rest of us could only dream about.

For example, he convinced his wife to drive their very fancy

THE TUESDAY MORNING GANG ANTHOLOGY

Chrysler convertible with a tow rope attached to the back. On the other end of the tow rope was Mr. Brown, seated in his glider. That was Brown's method of launching his glider airborne over La Jolla.

Unfortunately for Mr. Brown, the local authorities totally lacked enthusiasm for his pursuit of gliding aircraft in and around La Jolla.

Ever resourceful, and not lacking for the funds to fly around the country, Mr. Brown headed back to our nation's capital. There he managed to convince the Cabinet member who was in charge of the US Department of the Interior that he had discovered the ideal location for launching gliders.

When Mister Brown returned to La Jolla, he was once again confronted by the local authorities when he prepared to launch his glider.

They were none too happy with Mister Brown, since they had already made it quite clear that his newfound hobby of piloting glider planes was not going to be practiced off their local ocean bluff.

That's when Woody's friend blew the doors off these local naysayers. He calmly produced a letter from the US Department of the Interior designating the area a permanent glider port.

Thus was born the iconic La Jolla glider facility!

According to Woody, Brown went on to design the first large catamarans in 1941 or 1942. Woody reports that Mr. Brown's son is still plying the family trade by operating the tourist catamarans off the Waikiki beaches.

———————

Woody is a terrific photographer. If you take a trip the short distance up to the marvelous California Surf Museum located at 312 Pier Way in Oceanside, you'll get to enjoy many of the outstanding surfing pictures that Woody has taken over the years.

As an aside, Woody has been a major contributor to the California Surf Museum since it originally opened.

Many years ago, Woody obtained a unique camera from a gentleman by the name of Doc Ball. It is a box camera encased in highly-polished wood. Woody states that the camera is now very valuable. I believe that it can currently be viewed at the California Surf Museum, on loan from Woody.

What makes Doc Ball's camera truly unique is its lens. Therein lies the wellspring of another whimsical story.

When Woody bought the camera from Doc Ball, the good Doc passed along the lens' history.

Apparently Doc Ball was seeking a very high-powered lens for his new box camera.

He ultimately came up with a solution. Guess where he found it? At the Los Angeles Coroner's Office, of course!

Doc Ball was a dentist. Given his profession, what the heck he was doing in the LA Coroner's Office totally escapes even my normally fertile imagination. However, that's where the darn lens came from.

However, now that I have had an opportunity to ruminate further on the subject, maybe I have a solution to this conundrum.

It's like Duh!

The gentleman who had possession of the desired camera

lens apparently worked for the LA Coroner's Office. The deal they worked out was that the lens would be traded for a new gold tooth provided by Doc Ball for the Coroner's Office employee!

You think maybe that employee was a dental patient of Doc Ball and the subject somehow came up while he was treating that gentleman as a patient?

It works for me.

The only question I'm still struggling with is whether the subject lens was considered excess equipment by the guy's boss or whether the gentleman happened to "temporarily borrow" said lens from the City of Los Angeles.

Oh well, there we have another historical mystery, originating in excess of a half century ago, that you and I may not be able to solve without enlisting the services of the NCIS.

————————

Woody bought his beachfront lot on Neptune in 1965 for $19,000. In 1972, when he had saved up enough money, Woody was able to build a home on the lot for $54,000. I didn't ask Woody how much his house is worth now. However, if I had to hazard a guess, I think that, should he decide to sell it now, he would probably receive at least 30 to 35 times what he paid for it!

At the time, Woody was working in Oceanside in a lumber-yard and was a very skilled handyman. He personally milled (in Woody's vernacular "ripped") the bats and the trim around the windows and doors for the house.

After Woody built the home and got settled in, you could always tell which house was his when you were walking on the beach. The reason was that he had a Hobie Cat, always at the ready, parked part way up his ocean bluff.

Speaking of the Leucadia beach, that reminds me of a very special Woody story about the origins of the California Surf Museum.

As Stuart Resor (a local architect, longtime local surfer, Woody automobile aficionado, who was instrumental in putting together our annual worldwide Woody gatherings at Moonlight Beach, who owns one really cool Woody station wagon, and is an all-round good surfer dude) recalls the situation, he was walking along the beach near the Grandview access stairs, when he spied our protagonist, Woody.

It was 1986.

Stuart reports that he suddenly had an epiphany. As Stuart put it, seeing Woody in his advanced years (Stuart's words) *[Stuart I have to take exception to your chronological assessment. My God that was more than 35 years ago and Woody was only 53 years of age. Given the fact that he's 89 as this is being written, he was just a young whippersnapper, at that time!]*, trundling along the beach with his surfboard, made him focus on the need to preserve the historic stories of the iconic surfers who have graced the waves along the California coast.

As Stuart put it, when he saw Woody:

> "It suddenly seemed to me that the early days of surfing were slipping behind us, and if he and others were interested, we could display old surfboards and photographs for future generations to see."

The upshot of all of this is that our hero therefore provided the stimulus for Stuart Resor, together with a group of other like-minded surfers, to become the original founders of the fabulous California Surf Museum.

Since its formation, Woody has been a strong and generous supporter of the Museum, as has been our own Mike Burner.

The Museum has had numerous celebratory events that have included Woody and his old surfing buddies, including the iconic likes of the premier surf photographer, Leroy Grannis, our own photographer extraordinaire Tom Keck, exceptional surfboard shaper and manufacturer Dale Velzy, Phil Edwards, who brought balletic moves to surfing, and other such surfing luminaries.

As an aside, I can give testimony based upon my personal observations of Woody, that there is no one who is a more loyal and kind lifelong friend than Mr. Ekstrom. In his last days, Leroy Grannis ended up in an elder care facility, enjoying very few visitors.

That is, with the exception of Woody. Woody was a frequent visitor with Leroy right up until the time of his passing.

To finish up this piece, I was thinking of an expansive visit to Woody's well-earned reputation as the Lothario of Leucadia. However, since I was reminded that this is a PG version of Woody's life, I decided not to devote any ink to Woody's ongoing escapades, into his late 80s, with the fairer sex.

As I have quietly suggested to the august members of our group, those stories would have to be restricted to the X-rated version of these biographies, with distribution limited to the members only.

Definitely not to their families!

- nine -

Tom Keck

Tom didn't start out in either the LA South Bay or in La Jolla. Therefore, like a couple of us, including your author, Tom was a bit of an outlier relative to his geographical pedigree, which would normally disqualify him from membership in this august body.

However, Tom made up for that deficiency with his surfing creds, photographic skills, and being such an all-round bitch'n guy.

Before I undertook the task of writing about Tom, I asked him if he could provide me with a brief biography. His lame excuse was that he couldn't type. Instead he insisted on showing off by handing me a recent edition of *Ocean Magazine* that just happened to feature a cover story about Tom and his surfing photographs. It took me a little bit of time, but eventually I got over this over-the-top, vainglorious approach to my simple request for a bio. *[Just kidding, Tom]*

I then compounded the error by Googling Tom's name and ended up with a bio with all kinds of Adonis-type pictures of Tom as a young man, not to mention some of his iconic surf photographs, in the *Encyclopedia of Surfing*.

I must make an admission. This whole business of writing about our Tuesday Morning Gang is really getting depressing for me. Much to my surprise and, quite frankly, envy, when I Google the names of some of the members of our group, I find lots of information.

I use the term "envy" because when I Google my own name, about the only personal information I come up with is a location map for my law office that I closed 12 years ago!

By Googling, I can find autobiographical information on my family's original ancestor who came to this country from England in 1635. I can also find autobiographical information about my ancestor, the original Charles Marvin, who was born in 1804. The one and the same gentleman whose gaze glowers down upon me every day from his portrait hung on the wall of my office.

But all I can find out about myself is where my law office was located 12 years ago when I closed it!

Oh well, with the Tuesday Morning Gang, it is a bit of a burden to be around so many accomplished people, but I'll try to work through it.

Where were we? Oh yeah, we were talking about Tom Keck.

Tom was born on Coronado a lot of years ago. I'll give you a hint about his age. He's one year older than I am.

Tom's career as a Waterman started when he was a kid. He was body surfing as a youngster and had learned to ride his surfboard by the age of 14.

The photography bug began nibbling at Tom's derrière when he was in high school. He obtained an older 35mm camera and began taking photos of his high school friends.

He got serious about photography after he went away to college in Hawaii.

He chose to attend college at BYU's Hawaii campus, on the windward shore of Oahu. The reason was its proximity to North Shore surfing. From the college campus, it only took short trips to reach Sunset Beach and the Banzai Pipeline. *[As an aside, we are going so far back into ancient surfing history with Mr. Keck that those two world-famous surf spots hadn't even been named yet!]*

In the late 1950s, while attending BYU, Tom and his good friend, Tom Carlin, were filmed surfing by Bruce Brown, the iconic surfing moviemaker. The two of them were filmed by Brown for his surfing movie, *Barefoot Adventure* (1960).

According to the *Encyclopedia of Surfing* article I reviewed, in the movie Tom and his buddy were introduced as "two Mormon missionary surfers."

Although Tom isn't a Mormon, Bruce Brown never missed an opportunity to make funny on film.

After their introduction, Tom and his buddy were filmed in their missionary uniforms, drinking beer!

———————

Before I go any further, there is a mystery that I have to clear up with Tom after I first tried to write about the conundrum. *[Yeah, there's no doubt about it. I'm definitely of the ready, fire, aim genre of writing.]*

The mystery is this.

As I was going through the materials about Tom, it appeared to me that he spent considerable time in Hawaii going to college at BYU and working as a photographer during the period from 1955 through the early 1960s.

The confusion, and therefore the mystery, is the fact that when I was looking through old surfing materials, I found an *Ocean Magazine* article about the history of San Diego County lifeguards.

There is a specific portion of that coverage about our boy, Tom.

In the caption at the beginning of the article, they talk about Tom being a seasonal lifeguard from 1956 through 1964. I have no problem with his working for San Diego County as a lifeguard from 1956 through about 1959 or 1960. However, after college, if he was living full-time in Hawaii in the early 60s, how the heck was Tom a seasonal summer lifeguard in San Diego, through the year 1964?!

I'm sure Tom will have an explanation for this chronological confusion on my part.

However, while we're on the subject of Tom's lifeguard work, let's talk about what he allegedly did during that nine year period.

The way Tom explained it, he was a seasonal lifeguard because he could go to school during the winter and then come home, and still have a job in the summertime.

Let me see if I have this straight. Tom spent his summers on the San Diego County beaches as a seasonal lifeguard and his winters surfing on the North Shore. Have I got it right?

In any event, Tom apparently enjoyed some pretty interesting company while performing his lifeguard duties.

For example, he worked with the legendary Dempsey Holder and his brother, along with other lifeguard luminaries, manning the Imperial Beach lifeguard station.

Fortuitously for Tom, a photograph accompanied the magazine article which showed Tom and Dempsey checking out a surfboard. Lacking that photo, I might've had some reservations about his claim.

Tom cited as a fun memory the time he and Dempsey spotted a killer whale off the beach. Dempsey told him that he wanted to take a closer look at the leviathan via their rescue skiff.

They ended up following the whale in the rescue boat as it headed for the Tijuana sloughs. Tom related that the whale had its dorsal fin bent over, so Dempsey immediately dubbed him "Broken Fin."

Tom rued the fact that he didn't have a camera to record the historic event.

Fortunately for Tom, he was transferred to the County Lifeguard Headquarters in Solana Beach. The transfer occurred when the Imperial Beach beaches became overly polluted because of untreated sewage flow from Tijuana.

At the Solana Beach lifeguard station, Tom got to work with another famous local lifeguard, Captain Bill Rumsey. Rumsey had begun his lifeguarding career in the early 1930s.

At the Solana Beach station, he also got to work with a gentleman by the name of Red Shade. Mr. Shade was a great jazz musician. He was an accomplished guitar and banjo player. According to Tom, Shade would be playing and singing jazz, and Tom would tell Red: "You keep playing music, I'll watch the swimmers!"

As an aside, I'd venture a guess that Tom didn't just watch the swimmers. He obviously also kept a sharp eye on all of the young lovelies who gathered around the lifeguard tower to listen to Red play his banjo! *[I have a picture of that too!]*

Working out of the Solana Beach headquarters, he was also assigned to the Moonlight Beach lifeguard station. Tom reported that while he was working there, he got to watch Linda Benson and Rusty Miller become world-class surfers.

Tom also worked at Cardiff beach with Dempsey's brother, Mickey Holder.

Holder was an interesting character and another lifeguard legend. He was a World War II hero. When he returned from the war he started working as a San Diego City and County lifeguard in the 1940s. His lifeguarding career extended all of the way into the 1990s. For a good portion of his career, he had the unique opportunity of being the lifeguard in charge at Swamis.

In addition, Tom worked out of the lifeguard station at South Carlsbad State Beach (Ponto Beach). While at that station, Tom worked with Bill Hunt and a fellow by the name of Neil Tobin.

Tom and Mr. Hunt were delighted to have Tobin working with them because he was, in Tom's words, a super-deep sea diver. That attribute was important because, during their lifeguard shifts, he would often bring the two of them lobster and abalone that he had been out diving for, as their lunch!

Tom also worked at the Del Mar lifeguard station located at 25th Street. This is where, once again in Tom's words, he "kept an eye on Harry James and Doris Day frolicking in the surf."

Any doubts I may have had about Tom's lifeguard days were pretty much allayed by some photos I've come across.

First we had the picture with Dempsey Holder that I mentioned earlier. Then a photo credit to Tom for a photograph showing one of the San Diego County lifeguards surfing at Swamis.

However, the real clincher was the incredible photograph taken by Tom, "circa 1964," of the assembled San Diego County lifeguards at the Solana Beach headquarters. In that photograph, the lifeguards look like émigrés from a weightlifting team. No wimpy lifeguards in that group!

What's terrific about Tom's photograph is that it includes so many of the legendary San Diego County lifeguards.

So how did our Tom become so focused on being a photographer?

In some information which he actually did provide me, Tom indicated that in college he was working on a teaching credential. He decided to take a photography class because he claimed that he didn't know what he was doing when he was shooting film with his 35mm camera.

Actually, Tom ended up in the photography class by indirection. He needed a chemistry class in the pursuit of his college degree. He discovered that the college's curriculum included a class entitled, "The Chemistry of Photography."

Armed with that single college class in photography, he began focusing more on experimenting with his camera work. He found that his own backyard, the surf break at Pupukea, was a perfect location to hone his photographic skills.

It is interesting that when he started out, Tom shot mostly in black and white. The reason was that his finances would not support constantly using Kodachrome film. As he explained it, he only occasionally used colored film when the surf was really big.

Not only was the cost of the film daunting from a financial standpoint, but developing his camera shots was also quite expensive.

Still operating on a shoestring budget, Tom cut out the middleman and did his own film developing. In order to achieve that objective, he set up a darkroom in his home's only bathroom. That placed a heavy premium on timing his daily bathroom visits!

It appears that Tom was torn between his college class work and taking time to shoot surfing photographs. However, he did state that the choice got very simple when the surf was ginormous.

As Tom stated, then he decided to go for it and he began taking iconic surfing shots. He figured that he would worry about the classes later. Photography, and particularly surf photography, became his priority.

That same year Tom bought a surfboard from Pat Curren. This was at the time when pioneer surfers like Phil Edwards were beginning to master the iconic surfing spots such as Pipeline. However, Tom personally still preferred to body surf.

You have to remember when this was. It was back in a time when the North Shore of Hawaii was still a fairly isolated and quiet area that hadn't quite been "discovered" yet.

Being at the right place at the right time, his wonderful photographs gave Tom an opportunity to memorialize the early days of big wave riding and the incredible risk takers who initially challenged those monster waves.

I was really taken by a statement about Tom by Chris Ahrens, which appeared in the *Ocean Magazine*. In that portion of the article, Chris sought to explain why Tom has been so successful in working with the world's best surfers in his photography. As the article stated:

> "One thing that separates Tom Keck's work from most others is the comfort of his subjects. That's because Tom is a trusted friend to many of his photographic subjects and has a knack of nearly disappearing behind the lens."

When I read that quote, I was reminded of watching Tom one Tuesday morning casually, and very quietly, taking candid pictures of members of our gang. Once again, because Tom is our trusted friend, he did seem to disappear behind his camera lens.

In addition to Tom's surfing photographic work, while he was still in Hawaii he began to engage in commercial photographic work. He started doing freelance photography work for the two Honolulu newspapers because, in his words, "I was right on the spot when things happened."

Hearing those words, I'm reminded of Tom's amazing photograph which he has entitled, "Tanks for the Memories…" That is not a misspelling. It's his fascinating shot of the California National Guard tank facing off on the freeway with about 20 Sheriffs' police squad cars.

More on that little photographic adventure later.

———————

John Severson, who was the founder of *Surfer Magazine,* then enlisted Tom as a contributing photographer to his fledgling magazine.

Tom went on to become the magazine's main guy (Tom's words) for a few years until he left the islands because he had to return to California to attend to family matters.

———————

But before leaving the Hawaiian Isles, Tom had one other distinction that I recently learned about at one of our Tuesday morning meetings.

The subject came up when Don Hansen came by with his shopping cart and kibbitzed with our group for a bit. Don periodically shows up at our meetings in that manner.

After Don left, Tom, who happened to be sitting next to me when Don was visiting, leaned over to me and posed a question.

He inquired whether I was aware of where Don Hansen started his dynastic surfboard manufacturing career. In response, I mumbled something like I assume it was somewhere in the Cardiff or Encinitas areas.

"Nope," Tom said, "he started shaping surfboards in my garage in Hawaii, while my family and I were still in the islands."

Tom also shared another story about when Don Hansen and he were serving together as lifeguards in Del Mar. However, even though the statute of limitations has definitely run, I promised Tom I wouldn't include those details in this telling of his life story.

Suffice it to state that, for the benefit of Mr. Hansen, this little episode involved the liberation of a sizable length of copper conduit from public property, with the divestiture successfully completed employing the services of their lifeguard Jeep.

And that's all that's going to be said about that subject!

After he got back to our fair shores, Tom continued shooting surf shots that appeared in *Surfer Magazine*. In addition, Tom was a photographic contributor to a number of surfing magazines, including *International Surfing, Surf Guide, Surfing Illustrated, Surfer's Journal, Surfing World,* and *Pacific Longboarder,* among others.

Time magazine has even published Tom's photographs!

Tom opened a studio in Del Mar in the mid-1960s. He worked in the studio until he sold it in 1970. At that time, Tom decided that he was happier when he could spend his time being outside shooting surf pictures or photographs for news outlets.

Fortunately for the sustenance of Tom's family, at the time when he sold the studio, Tom was hired for a full-time photographic job with the San Diego ABC TV station.

In Tom's words, he was hired as a full-time news photographer:

> " . . . with a car, gas card and all of the benefits that
> took care of my wife and kids. Ah, life is good!"

Tom did have a serious blow to his career in 1978. While he was out on a storm damage assignment, his home was flooded.

That flooding resulted in the destruction of almost all of Tom's surf photo negatives and transparencies.

Can you imagine coming home and being confronted with the destruction of almost two decades of your life's work?!

———————

In the late 1980s, Tom started having back problems, which led to a major back operation. In 1988 he had to go on medical disability because of his back. The back problem was so severe that Tom was forced to spend a year in bed.

Imagine having to go through that miserable experience when you are an outdoor guy like Tom!

———————

Because of his weakened back, Tom had to make another shift in his photographic career. He no longer was able to carry the heavy 16mm and video TV gear. Tom decided to once again fall back on his still photographic skills.

That led him to stints working for the *San Diego Union/Tribune* and the *LA Times,* San Diego Bureau. His work with the *LA Times* lasted until 1993, when they shut down the San Diego Bureau. However, he still got to work for the *Times* after that.

In 1996, the *Times* work included Tom's photographic coverage of the Republican National Convention in San Diego. Tom indicated to me that he made a lot of money on that two-week assignment.

———————

As I indicated, I've seen just enough of Tom's photographs to want to see a lot more.

Keeping in mind my limited exposure to Tom's photographic work, in addition to the terrific picture of the Coronado Surf Club members, my other personal favorite is his "Tanks for the Memories" photograph.

Those of us that were around in 1995 when Tom took the shot remember the horror of watching TV reports about some nutcase stealing a very large and very dangerous California National Guard tank.

Once he had control of the tank, he wreaked havoc with the behemoth by smashing and driving over parked vehicles, doing extensive property damage, and scaring the be-Jesus out of anyone in the neighborhood of where he was operating the tank.

The police squad cars immediately reacted when they were alerted of the wacko conducting his version of an urban demolition derby.

However, their police vehicles were no match for the tank. All they could do was follow the rampaging tank.

Because of his work as a news photographer, Tom told me he monitored police channels in his car. After hearing about the chaotic tank event, Tom began monitoring the police channels to determine where the tank was headed next.

He ultimately determined from the police radio chatter that the tank was likely to get on the freeway. Quick-thinking Tom decided to try to get ahead of the action at a freeway overpass. He tried one, but realized he wouldn't get the shot he was seeking. He then raced to the next freeway offramp, got up on the freeway overpass, and using a long lens, set up his memorable photograph.

In the photograph, he was shooting towards the four lanes of southbound 805, in the vicinity of the 163 offramp.

The tank was headed towards Tom with a phalanx of about 20 police squad cars arrayed across the freeway, confronting the tank.

I don't recall exactly what happened after Tom took his picture. I do know that the police finally succeeded in stopping the tank. Then one of the officers got on top of the tank and shot down into the tank's interior, killing the tank's operator.

Not surprisingly, because it was such an incredible story, Tom told me that his photograph of the tank was included in national news media coverage.

Since his days as a news photographer, Tom has turned his focus back to his surfing photographic works. Unfortunately, I don't think I knew Tom 11 years ago. I say unfortunately, because in 2006 at the California Surf Museum in Oceanside, they had a retrospective of Tom's work entitled: "Tom Keck: Exposed." Sure would've liked to personally have had a chance to enjoy that photographic retrospective.

Tom related that recently there has been quite a demand from foreign magazines for his surfing photos.

That's the good news. According to Tom, the bad news is that it costs an arm and a leg to send photos out of the country.

Nowadays, Tom's primary effort is to gather his surfing photos taken over so many years and making certain that they are properly catalogued in the Heritage Surfing Museum, where the majority of his photographic work is being preserved.

Sadly, as I noted, I haven't had an opportunity to see that many of Tom's surfing masterpieces. Hopefully, I'll have an opportunity in the future to see a lot more.

However, the strong feeling I get from Tom's surfing photos that I have seen is the basic humanity of his shots.

Whether you're looking at Tom's 1996 photo of Chris Dixon, wiping out at the Newport Wedge in front of a large audience on the beach and the belly boarder at the bottom of the wave, looking back up in horror at Dixon's imminent peril; his wonderful 1963 shot of Mike Turkington surfing a giant wave in front of two young ladies sitting on the beach at Yokohama Bay, on the west side of Oahu; the 1963 Waimea Bay photo of the legendary Hawaiian surfer, Kimo Hollinger, ripping down a monster wave; or the incredible Coronado Surf Club shot by Tom in 1962 over a tidepool reflecting the club members and their Woodies on the other side, the humanity of the subjects leaps off the photograph right at the viewer.

That humanity also shines through in timeless photos like the one of Miki Dora in 1966, in his formal black tuxedo, at the International Surfing Hall of Fame in Hollywood, wearing flowered tennis shoes! Miki was a little ahead of his time with his tennis shoes and tux.

Tom's compassion and good will also radiate from his pictures of Duke Kahanamoku in 1966, being inducted into the Surfing Hall of Fame, and Rell Sunn, on the beach before a paddle out honoring Eddie Aikau, at his Memorial Surfing Contest in 1993.

———

However, the surf shot taken by Tom that probably brought him the most worldwide exposure, was a photograph that also earned Tom what he thought would be the lifelong enmity of Hobie Alter.

This was Tom's famous 1962, "Broken Board at Sunset Beach," photograph.

The photograph depicts a very buff young man standing on the sand at Sunset Beach, holding with his left arm, the nose half of his surfboard, and with his right arm, the tail section of the gigantic board. The board must've been at least 11 feet long and very wide and thick. It had clearly broken in half during the surfer's wave riding. That was back in the day when surfboards were built like tanks and they just flat didn't break in half.

Again in Tom's words, the photograph was:

" . . . an around the world shot that United Press International (UPI) picked up and made me, at a young college-age, almost famous. The unlucky owner is a fireman from Rockaway Beach, New York. The bad part for me was it was a Hobie board, and Hobie was pissed when he saw the morning paper. No board got broken in those days, and Hobie was on the phone to Dick Metz in Honolulu at the Hobie outlet. We became friends much later in life."

Tom told me that when Hobie made that telephone call to Dick Metz, he was one angry hombre. Tom heard about it from Metz, and he thought that Hobie would never get over Tom's inadvert effort at eclipsing Hobie's storied career with one click of his camera lens.

However, at a later (much later!) gathering of surfers, Tom

and Hobie managed to patch up their relationship, in spite of Tom's earlier inadvertent torpedo attack on Hobie's run at surfing and Hobie Cat immortality.

In closing this brief piece about Tom and his amazing photographic journey, I would like to again quote from Chris Ahrens' article about Tom, in *Ocean Magazine:*

> "While many of his peers had made bigger names for themselves in the surfing world, he continues to do what he's always done – shoot the photos that define our lives and times. So take your time and look closely into the corners, where 1950s style bathing suits and military crew cuts reveal another time, or back to the future with the longboard renaissance and the walk-on-water majesty of an endless nose ride. Keck's large body of work speaks of perfection, dedication, timing and passion, capturing the waves of our lives for nearly six decades."

A well-earned tribute to our Tom!

- ten -
Charles "Chuck" V. Lindsay II, M.D.

Yep, the Tuesday Morning Gang even has its own doctor, Chuck Lindsay. Doctor, surfer, fisherman, pilot extraordinaire, counselor, and all-around good guy.

And Chuck is first and foremost the real deal when it comes to a North San Diego County guy. As a matter of fact, he still lives in the home where he was literally born, in Leucadia!

Chuck's dad was the first full-time Encinitas doctor who came and stayed in Encinitas. And, after other moving around during WWII, he and his family stayed for the rest of his life.

There is a back story about how Chuck's mom and dad found Encinitas as their permanent home.

In February 1926, they were on a camping trip from their home in Santa Barbara, in their Model T Ford. They stopped in Encinitas to see what the need might be for a doctor serving the San Dieguito area.

Their first stop in the area was at the Westbrook Hardware Store, in "downtown" Encinitas. Fortunately, when they went into the store, they ended up talking to the owner, Mr. Westbrook.

They explained to him that they were camping. Feeling sorry for them, Mr. Westbrook asked: "You're camping in all this rain, are you?" When Chuck's dad answered in the affirmative, Mr. Westbrook invited his dad, mom, and their newborn baby, Chuck's older sister Joanne, to camp in his stockroom as long as they needed.

His mom and dad quickly determined that they really liked Encinitas and decided to move here in July 1926.

Chuck's dad opened a medical office in downtown Encinitas, which was next to the saloon, and across Hwy. 101 from the Encinitas Hotel. He occupied this office from 1926 through 1937. His office location is presently the retail store known as "Queen Eileen's."

Thus Encinitas, not to mention the San Dieguito area, not only had its first permanent doctor, but that doctor came fully equipped with a nurse who happened to be his wife, and Chuck's mom!

———————

Chuck's mom and dad built their first home in Leucadia at 133 La Veta. As Chuck notes, the medical practice was going well, and with the arrival of Chuck's sister Elaine in May 1928, they needed an expanded residence.

Chuck's dad then built a second home at 304 La Veta, two blocks north of the first one. This was the home where Chuck's Mom and Dad raised their family and lived in until they sold it to Chuck in 1966.

Chuck has lived there ever since.

———————

Since Chuck strikes me as the kind of guy who never does things in half measure, his arrival on this earthly realm was no different.

On September 17, 1931, Chuck's mom went into labor with him. Unfortunately for his mom, at that time Chuck's dad was off someplace delivering another baby in Leucadia.

Now we're dealing with a mom who was about to deliver, and who had 12 brothers and sisters when she was brought up on a dry farm in Eastern Kansas. Those types of Kansans are hardy folk. Not only that, but Chuck's mom was a well-trained nurse in the art of birthing.

So did Chuck's mom panic at the pending birth without her doctor husband? No way!

She contacted a neighbor lady to come help her. She had already prepared the birthing room with all the necessities. Since Chuck was her third birth, he made a rather quick exit.

By the time his dad got home from delivering the other baby, he was a father for the third time. Upon his arrival, Chuck's mom was all freshened up after having given birth to Chuck.

Chuck's dad's first question was the gender of the baby. Since his mom knew he wanted a boy, she nonchalantly replied: "She's the cutest little girl you have ever seen!"

Chuck's dad didn't take her at her word. He immediately marched in, checked the baby's diaper, and found that in fact he did have the boy that he wanted so badly.

One of Chuck's dad's first friends when he moved Encinitas was Paul Ecke Sr., who had moved from Hollywood as a farmer to Saxony Boulevard, in Encinitas, to grow poinsettias. They were lifelong friends.

In the early 1930s, the local kids went to the high school in Oceanside by wagon and other rather archaic conveyances. Seeing that as a problem that needed to be solved, Chuck's dad got together with some other local men and by 1934 they had begun construction on the new San Dieguito High School, on Santa Fe Drive, in Encinitas.

———————

During the war years, since Chuck's mom and dad were moving around so much because his dad was an officer in the military, Chuck was put in a private school at the Academy for Loma Linda University.

Chuck made amazingly swift work of high school and college, because he finished both in 7 years, graduating from Loma Linda University at only 20 years of age.

Since he was quite comfortable at Loma Linda, he then went to their medical school and finished his initial medical training, graduating with his medical degree when he was only 24 years of age.

After he got his medical degree, Chuck obtained an internship position in Lansing, Michigan, with a mentor who was an orthopedic surgeon. At the time, Chuck was interested in becoming an orthopedic surgeon, possibly working in OB/GYN, or as a urologist.

However, after tagging along with his mentor into a number of court trials where he was sued for malpractice, Chuck told his mentor that he wanted to spend his time practicing medicine and not being a denizen of the courtrooms!

———————

On the surfing front, Chuck, being a Leucadia boy through and through, decided when he was a young teenager that he wanted to surf. He made his surfboards himself. He still owns the drawknife he shaped his boards with.

Since there were no shapers here in Encinitas, he shaped his first board out of redwood. According to Chuck, it was a classic Duke Kahanamoku surfboard. Chuck stated that it was one heavy sucker, weighing in at about 95 pounds!

Then Chuck made his next surfboard, which was a semi-hollow redwood board. The next board he made was a balsa strip board. It was a beaut.

Because he was away at boarding school during his later teenage years, he was only able to surf in the summertime.

His favorite surfing beach was Cardiff Reef. Because his initial boards were so big and heavy, he couldn't surf the shore break and had to find an outside reef break. For that reason, he favored Cardiff Reef.

He would've liked to have surfed at Swamis, but back in the 1940s there was no easy public access. You could only gain access to the Swami's surf break from the Self Realization Fellowship property or around the point at Cardiff Reef.

Later on, when the surf got big, he headed south to Windansea. On other occasions he headed north to San Onofre or Trestles for his surfing.

———

Chuck first got interested in flying when he was 15 years old. Maybe it was even earlier. The reason is that one of the first things Chuck remembers from his childhood is a swing in their yard made into an airplane, with wings, seat and tail. According to Chuck, he spent a heck of a lot of time between the ages of 3 and 5 on that airplane swing.

Chuck's love of flying led him into an amazing number of adventurous flights as he racked up more than 11,600 flight hours in small aircraft.

I want to share with you three of those adventures. A trip to Alaska with his dad that was suggested by his dad. Another trip of 31 days, also suggested by his dad, who accompanied him, all over South America. The last is a local story, but a wonderful demonstration of our Doc's flying skills.

Local flying story first.

Chuck recently shared with me a rather incredible story about an aircraft landing on Leucadia's alternate airfield landing strip at night, without landing lights or an operating engine.

This landing strip has none of the usual amenities for airfields. It has no marked runway, runway lights, control tower, taxiways, and the like. As a matter of fact, its use is limited to a random landing every couple of decades or so.

That's probably a good thing.

The reason is that we're talking about landing on the beach!

A couple years ago there was a forced landing by an aircraft on the beach in Carlsbad near Palomar Airport Road. The aircraft had been towing a banner, had a mechanical, and made a semi-controlled crash landing on a crowded beach. Unfortunately, a child playing on the beach was hit by the plane and suffered injuries.

I'm glad to report that the story I'm about to relate did not involve any injuries, although, frankly, it's an absolute miracle that no one got hurt.

The incident involved Chuck himself. It occurred in 1963.

Chuck, along with some other gentlemen who worked at Tri-City Hospital, had a flying club.

According to Chuck, because none of the members of the club were overly wealthy, the maintenance records on the planes that the club purchased were somewhat spotty.

On this particular occasion, they had taken the aircraft down to Gillespie Field to have repairs made to the plane's radio.

At the time Chuck was in his early 30s. Fortunately for all concerned, prior to that particular night, he had had quite a bit of flying experience.

The folks flying in the plane included Chuck, the first Administrator for the Tri-City Hospital, Chuck's girlfriend, and her two children; and of course I need to mention the children's two dachshund dogs.

After they had received word from Gillespie Field that the plane was ready, they all drove down to fly the airplane back up to Palomar Airport. Everyone anticipated it would be a fun little airplane ride.

Little did they realize the aerial adventure that they were about to embark on.

When they were preparing to get into the aircraft at Gillespie Field, the Administrator asked Chuck if he could pilot the plane for the short trip back to the North County.

At the time it was dark and the other fellow was not qualified for night flying. In other words, he wasn't IFR (Instrument Flight

Regulations) qualified. If the truth be known, the gentleman had never flown a plane at night before. As a matter fact, prior to that evening, he had only 38 hours of flight time!

However, Chuck thought it would be good practice for him, and given the fact that Chuck, a very experienced pilot, was sitting in the right seat, he agreed to let the Administrator pilot the plane.

Everything went pretty smoothly with the flight until they reached a point just north of Solana Beach.

At that juncture, to quote Chuck, "the engine swallowed a valve."

Even for those of you who are not aviation aficionados, like myself, that probably doesn't sound like a good thing. And it wasn't!

Turns out the escaping valve got trapped inside the engine casing and cracked the casing. When that occurred, the result was something that will ruin a pilot's day, even if he's flying a multi-engine plane. However, it is particularly concerning when you're flying a plane with a single engine and the propeller suddenly stops turning.

With the open crack in the engine housing, oil began to leak. Chuck said he could smell the oil burning, which is not an olfactory experience that you look forward to when you're an aviator.

The reason is that the next event that usually follows, as day follows night, is a fire. Aviation fires, especially those occurring while you're flying, are not particularly favored within the aviation community.

Fortunately for Chuck and his beleaguered crew, a fire didn't break out.

Of course the engine on the plane immediately quit after the valve was swallowed by the engine. Because the Administrator was an inexperienced pilot, his knee-jerk reaction was to try to pull up the nose of the newly- converted glider plane.

Not a good idea.

When your engine quits and you pull up the nose of the aircraft, you immediately risk experiencing wing stall. If that occurs, one or both of your aircraft wings will fall through and your aircraft will quickly assume a vertical orientation with the nose of the plane headed irrevocably towards terra firma.

To enhance the E-ticket ride possibilities, when your aircraft assumes the nose-down position, there is also a high likelihood that your aircraft will go into a spin.

Therefore, on balance, pulling up the nose of the aircraft was not the best solution that night for dealing with the engine quitting.

Fortunately for all concerned, Chuck immediately instructed the inexperienced pilot to bring the aircraft's nose back down.

At that juncture, the Administrator did the most prudent thing that he could think of, given all of the circumstances. And he probably took at least a millisecond to make this decision.

He took his hands off the controls and yelled to Chuck: "Chuck, you got it!

Good call Sir! Under the circumstances, in dealing with

an aircraft emergency, Chuck's some 3,000 hours of pilot time rather easily trumped your 38 hours of flying experience!

[As an aside, Chuck doesn't fly anymore, but before he quit flying he had accumulated approximately 11,600 incredible hours of pilot time! All of this flying time was accumulated in small private planes.]

———

Where were we? Oh I remember, we were somewhere just north of Solana Beach in a single engine plane that had suddenly been converted into a reluctant glider. For the uninitiated, this type of aircraft was not designed for, nor was it particularly suited for, the gliding mode of flight.

If the truth be told, the glide characteristics of this aircraft were probably just a cut above a rock.

Once Chuck took control of the aircraft and got the nose back down to accommodate the optimum glide angle, his newly-anointed copilot looked down at Coast Highway 101, below their flight path, and suggested to Chuck that they land on the highway.

Chuck took one look down at all the automobile traffic lights and immediately responded that there were too many cars on the Highway to attempt to use it as a landing field, unless his new copilot was suggesting that they attempt to land on top of an automobile. (Acknowledgement: I made up that wise apple remark.)

———

At about this juncture in the evening's adventures, pure, unmitigated, serendipity took charge.

First and foremost, you had the perfect pilot manning the controls.

To state that Chuck loves everything about aviation and flying would be a gross understatement.

Here's a guy who decided to become a doctor so that he would have sufficient money to be able to afford to fly planes.

As a matter of fact, after he had received his medical residency training, he agreed to join the Navy Medical Corps because he received orders to be sent to the Naval Air Station, Pensacola, Florida, to receive flight training to become qualified as a Naval Aviator.

The Navy's intent was to qualify him as a Naval Aviator and, because of his medical pedigree, designate him a flight surgeon. Unfortunately for Chuck, because of a cutback in US defense spending, that dream didn't pan out.

Even today, many years after his flying career ended, he spends all of his spare time reading about hundreds of old aircraft. He just can't get enough of the stuff.

In other words, in the midst of this potentially horrendous aviation catastrophe, at the flight controls you had a gentleman who possessed "the right stuff" to pull off the minor aviation miracle which was required.

The second critical factor contributing to the good fortune of the occupants of that wounded aircraft was that Chuck was so familiar with the North Coast area of San Diego. Although he had just returned from serving in the Navy, because he had spent so much time during his younger days around the North Coast, he had critical knowledge of the area's geography and topography.

When Chuck took over the controls, the first thing he did was set up the airplane for the maximum glide path.

Once Chuck had the aircraft in a controlled glide, he began to engage in some rapid strategic planning about where he was going to place the aircraft when it came back to earth.

Part of that planning effort involved checking his avionics to determine whether or not he could restart the airplane's engine. When he made that decision, Chuck wasn't aware of the major extent of the actual damage to the aircraft's engine.

At this point in the narrative, your scribe is approaching alien territory. I know enough about flying to be able to, often with some difficulty, strap on my seatbelt, and that's about it.

Chuck indicated that he reached down under the pilot seat and inadvertently hit the master electrical switch in an effort to try to restart the aircraft's engine. Unfortunately, when he hit the switch, it turned off all the power in the airplane so that Chuck was flying completely blind, without instruments or landing lights.

To add to his challenges, Chuck stated that it was a completely moonless night and black as pitch outside the aircraft

At the time when the engine quit, he guesses that the aircraft was between 2,300 and 3,000 feet in altitude. He did some quick calculations on how far the aircraft would glide.

His first conclusion was that they would not be able to reach an airfield for the landing.

He then decided that his only hope was to put the aircraft down on the beach.

Based upon his rough calculations of the aircraft glide path and the fact that he didn't really have any other options, he

CHARLES "CHUCK" V. LINDSAY II, M.D.

determined that their return to Mother Earth was going to be in the vicinity of Moonlight Beach in Encinitas.

He also knew that there was a structure out on Moonlight Beach, with a light high up on the top of it, which would give him a point of reference as he was attempting to land the plane. In addition, the lights from the homes at the top of the beach bluff also gave him some points of reference on this moonless, extremely dark night.

However, of critical importance, there were no lights down on the beach itself and it was pitch black. Obviously the problem was compounded by not having any landing lights available. For those of you who have been down on our beaches at night, you have some sense of just how dark it gets.

As they were approaching Moonlight Beach, Chuck recognized that they were going to end up landing north of where the Moonlight Beach light would give him the reference point he wanted.

He considered turning the plane to shorten its glide path so he would be able to land at Moonlight. He quickly discarded that idea because he recognized that without power, if you drop a wing you would immediately lose altitude and there would be a high likelihood that they would auger in and crash.

Therefore, he kept going north along the beach and finally landed about 75 to 100 yards north of the Cottonwood Creek which runs out into the northern portion of the Moonlight Beach.

———————

When Chuck was making his approach to the final landing, it was so dark he could not differentiate between land and water.

Apparently Chuck made an incredible landing. He stated that he hardly felt the wheels hit the sand. He called it one of his best landings ever and, because of the darkness, he did it totally blind.

Chuck told me that probably the most critical thing that he did, immediately prior to the landing, was to pull full flaps on the aircraft. That maneuver is done by all pilots when they make a landing, and Chuck stated he didn't even think about it. He just automatically pulled full flaps, even though he couldn't tell precisely how close he was to the ground.

The effect of pulling flaps is to cause the airplane to flare, immediately prior to touchdown.

To get some idea of just how incredible the landing was, consider this.

When the aircraft finally came to rest, one wheel, the one closest to the bluff, was dry. The other wheel was wet from landing in the ocean.

The rest of the story of that night's perilous adventures could only have occurred during a different time than the present.

If this little escapade had occurred today, I'm sure that Chuck would end up spending a good year or two in the midst of various agency investigations. As it turned out, the only public official who gave them any trouble was the overzealous Sheriff's deputy who I will describe below.

For the adults in the plane, when they were safely on the ground and had started breathing normally again, they turned to Chuck and said something to the effect of: "How did you do that!?!" Chuck still just shrugs his shoulders when asked that question.

Of course, in all their childhood naïveté, the kids were not particularly impressed by the whole adventure.

The children had their priorities straight. As soon as they got out of the aircraft down on the beach, they proclaimed that they were hungry and wanted to know where they could eat!

Chuck's girlfriend had a friend in Leucadia, and they managed to get the kids and the dachshunds off to her house.

Chuck estimated that they had landed on the beach about mid-tide. The ever practical Chuck then was faced with the issue of getting his airplane quickly off the beach, before it started heading to Hawaii with the next high tide.

He managed to come up with the type of practical solution to this conundrum that today would never be permitted or sanctioned, given our overly-regulated lives.

Chuck had a friend who lived on the bluff next to the Stone Steps access (across the street from Jim Enright's home which was built much later). He knew that the friend had a Jeep.

He walked the couple of hundred yards up the beach to Stone Steps and went up the stairs and knocked on his friend's door.

When his friend came to the door, Chuck explained to him what had happened.

The friend's immediate reaction was to blurt out: "You've got to be kidding!!"

The friend agreed to loan Chuck his Jeep. Chuck hopped in the Jeep and next rounded up a cousin who lived nearby and a length of sturdy rope.

They managed to use the Jeep to very carefully tow the airplane back to Moonlight Beach. Chuck indicated they had to be careful, because it would've been very easy to damage the landing gear while they were towing the plane.

Fortunately at that time, more than a half century ago, there was a parking lot down close to beach level on the north side of Moonlight Beach. Using the Jeep, they were able to haul the plane up onto the automobile parking lot.

When they initially landed on the beach, there was no one around.

However, as you can imagine, by the time they managed to tow the airplane up onto the parking lot, they had attracted quite a bit of attention.

In addition to the usual neighborhood looky-loos, who gathered around the parked aircraft, they had managed to attract a San Diego County Sheriff, a State Park Ranger who was normally stationed in Carlsbad, and a CHP officer.

Early on in their conversations, Chuck told these individuals that in the morning he would get a flatbed truck and move the airplane out of the parking lot, back up to its normal domicile at the Oceanside Airport.

By the time Chuck finished his rather incredible narrative about how the airplane ended up where it was, the assembled governmental representatives all seemed satisfied, with one exception.

The exception was the San Diego County Sheriff's Deputy. In a very officious manner, the deputy proceeded to explain to Chuck that, after having checked the rulebook, he had determined that it was illegal to park an airplane in an automobile parking lot!! Therefore the deputy was going to have to issue Chuck a citation!

Chuck never did explain to me what the citation would have been for. Having the fertile imagination that I do, mixed in with about 40 years of the practice of law, I can conjure up all manner of possible bureaucratic silliness. Fortunately, however, I never pursued that issue with Chuck.

That evening, apparently cooler heads prevailed. The Deputy Sheriff was talked out of issuing some manner of citation to Chuck for parking his stricken airplane in a public automobile parking lot.

After the governmental representatives finally departed, Chuck went back up to his home on La Veta and brought back a camper shell which he parked next to the disabled aircraft.

On the way back to the beach, he stopped to pick up some rather large containers of vodka and rum, and the requisite mixers.

For the balance of the night, until the next morning, Chuck, his girlfriend, and his erstwhile copilot, whiled away the hours until sunrise inhaling voluminous amounts of alcohol, as they maintained sentry duty guarding their damaged airplane.

As Chuck had promised, the next morning they took the wings off the airplane and loaded the aircraft's fuselage and detached wings on a flatbed truck. They then hauled the disassembled aircraft back up to Oceanside Airport, where it was put back together.

So ends the saga about the use of Leucadia's alternate aircraft landing field.

The next flying adventure we're going to talk about involved a flying trip around Alaska.

In 1964 Chuck had purchased a brand-new, four seat, two engine Beechcraft Twin Comanche aircraft. It was the only new plane that Chuck ever bought. He said he felt guilty buying it, because after he had made a verbal agreement to use it for charter, a man from Rancho Santa Fe with a 6 Place Twin, made an arrangement with the first Fixed Base Operator at Palomar Airport, and that Twin was used almost exclusively. Therefore, without the expected income from the charter business, the monthly costs for the airplane really became uncomfortable.

When he voiced those concerns to his dad, Chuck said his dad had a surprising solution to the issue: "Let's take your new airplane up to Alaska."

Chuck and his dad, along with the same first Administrator for Tri-City Hospital, and Chuck's cousin, took off in Chuck's new plane for Alaska.

They ran into their first hairy situation when the Pacific Coast of Alaska was socked in by weather, and getting over the mountains to Anchorage was too risky. The route that they were expecting to travel would have involved flying at 8,000 feet, but there was reported ice forming at 5,500 feet. Therefore, they had to divert to a little town called Whittier.

All they had at Whittier was a gravel landing strip. The good news was that even though they landed at 11:30 at night, because it was in June, there was plenty of daylight.

The bad news was that the uphill gravel strip had rock berms on both sides of it. When Chuck tried to turn around to run his plane back down the landing strip, because the Twin Comanche has a low wing aspect, in some instances the boulders that were part of the berms on both sides were not much more than 1 foot under Chuck's airplane's wings!

I have a question for you Chuck: How in heaven's name did you land the plane in the first place with the berm boulders so close to your wingtips?!

As a side story, consider a very important factor that became critical the next day. The town of Whittier had been built up during World War II to act as a supply depot for war materials. According to Chuck, the primary reason why they built the Alaskan Highway and the second-longest tunnel in the world, ultimately accommodating railroad trains and cars, was to transport military equipment and supplies by rail to this little town of Whittier to supply the military bases on the Aleutian Chain during WWII.

In March of that same year, only a few months before Chuck's plane arrived in Whittier, Alaska had been devastated by the 9+ Richter scale earthquake and follow-on tsunami. As a matter of fact, a number of the buildings in Whittier had been wiped out by the earthquake and tsunami.

———

The next morning one of the locals suggested to Chuck that instead of using the very dangerous gravel runway to take off, he should take off from the main street of the town!

Chuck stated that after he inspected the main street, he realized that the buildings on opposite sides of the main Street were so far apart, and the roadway was so wide, that a takeoff with his plane was possible.

And take off he did, but not before holding the plane's nose down, prior to rotation on takeoff, to pass under three sets of power lines!

———

The white-knuckle takeoff from Whittier wasn't the end of the severe puckering which accompanied them in their flying that day.

Before they left Whittier, one of the local aviators advised Chuck that they would be passing through a bowl-shaped area at a higher altitude along their planned route. The gentleman advised Chuck that "when you get into that bowl, turn right" to take the pass to Anchorage.

Sounds like the old days of seat-of-the-pants, dead reckoning flying to me!

Anyway, as Chuck eased into that bowl area that he been warned about, suddenly he was in a total white out! They couldn't see a bloody thing!

So what did Chuck do?

This is a heavily guarded state secret and please keep it to yourself. However, he didn't have the option of going to his instruments. And even if he had been able to do that, his instruments probably wouldn't have told him where the far wall was in that bowl!

So he did the only thing he could do, which was follow instructions and turn right! According to Chuck, the Hospital Administrator, who was sitting in the copilot seat, was so unnerved by the entire episode that he locked onto the airplane's yoke.

He had the darned thing in a death grip until Chuck screamed at him to let go of the yoke!

At about this time, when things were looking as bleak as possible, Chuck thought he saw increased light off the nose of the plane. He immediately headed for that brighter spot and fortunately was successful in climbing out of that godforsaken bowl.

Chuck, being the Christian man that he is, corrected me. Instead of a godforsaken bowl, he noted the hand of God in giving him the light that led to their escape from an untimely demise!

But their day wasn't over yet. After that very scary interlude, they traveled on to Anchorage, Alaska, and landed about 9:30 a.m. at Merrill Field. It was an absolutely crystal-clear, beautiful day. At the airport they could see Denali, Alaska's iconic mountain, in the distance.

While they were refueling, they talked with a local. He made the suggestion that, if possible, it was the absolutely perfect day to fly around Denali.

Initially Chuck didn't think it was a good idea. His dad

had been suffering from heart disease, and when flying around Denali, they would be flying at an altitude of anywhere from 13,000 to 17,000 feet, without oxygen. However, his dad convinced him that he could handle it.

Apparently they were able to get some fantastic photographs of the mountain during their flight.

While they were flying around Alaska, Chuck and his dad talked about a trip that Chuck was planning to São Paulo, Brazil. The purpose of the trip was to attend the 3rd World Congress of Anesthesiologists.

Chuck explained that he was going to have to get to a travel agent to obtain commercial airline tickets to São Paulo for the convention.

Then his father, totally unexpectedly, pulled another rabbit out of his hat. He said to his son:

"Forget about the commercial flights. Let's fly your
Twin Comanche to the convention in São Paulo!"

And they did! Chuck had been worried about all of the visas and other administrative obligations that you had to deal with on a private plane trip like this. When he voiced his concern to his father, his dad said not to worry about it; he would take care of all that.

And he did.

Chuck has made casual passing mention of flying to South

America at our meetings. Since I was first titillated as a writer by that little morsel, I had been looking forward to sitting down with Chuck and reviewing that momentous trip.

The purpose of our getting together was to have Chuck give me his basic biographical information.

We sat together talking for 4½ hours. Probably 4 of those hours were devoted to Chuck and his dad's incredible 31-day Latin American flying adventures!

As I told Chuck during our meeting, if I were to write up a narrative that includes everything that happened in those 31 days, I would be presenting you folks with a short novel. Instead, I'm going to hit the high points of the trip below.

Let's cover the route they followed in their flying trip and pick up some stories along the way.

First of all, the airplane and the pilot. Chuck and his dad were flying in the Twin Comanche. Chuck had 7,000 to 8,000 hours of pilot flight time before they started the trip. However, Chuck wasn't instrument rated.

Having been around Navy squadrons for a while as a naval officer, if I was planning on being Chuck's passenger on that flight, I might've been a little nervous about the lack of an instrument rating on such a monumental flying trip.

But what do I know!?

The first legs of the trip were from San Diego down the Baja, and then across to mainland Mexico.

They then flew down across Mexico to the border of

Honduras. Next they flew across Honduras and landed in Nicaragua. After spending three nights on San Andres Island, they flew over Panama to Medellin, Colombia.

They then headed out to Quito but had to divert because of potential icing. They ended up on the West Coast of Columbia at Tumaco, near the Equator, where it was hotter than blazes. According to Chuck, the primary mode of travel in that area was in dugout canoes through the jungle rivers. The dugout canoes had a free board of about 2 or 3 inches, and had all manner of people and animals crowded on board.

When they arrived, they landed on a grassy runway which had so much moisture that for a bit Chuck was totally blinded during his landing by the water splatter.

They landed safely, but the water shorted out one of the plane's generators. They then flew over Ecuador, and the deserts of Peru, until they landed in Lima, Peru.

At that point, Chuck caught a real break. He knew he had to fix his generator because, although he had two of them on the plane, he didn't want to risk long-distance flying on one generator. As he was preparing to land, he talked with the controller who spoke English. *[By the way, according to Chuck, fortunately for him throughout this trip involving countries where the natives speak Spanish and Portuguese, English is the universal language at all Airport Towers.]*

He told the tower controller that his generator was out and he needed to get it repaired. He further told him that he had an acquaintance who worked for Pan Am in Lima. He asked the controller to contact his friend, and he did.

Shortly after the landing, the acquaintance and his mechanics met them at the plane and eventually had the repairs made.

Chuck was dreading the repair bill because he thought it would be pretty high. In reality, he was charged all of $29 for all of that work and materials!

––––––––––

They next wanted to fly from Lima to Cusco. *[Editor's Note: Machu Picchu is a 3-hour train ride from Cusco. I've taken that train and visited Machu Picchu. It was the most awe-inspiring place I've ever been to in my life!]*

After filing a flight plan with the intended destination of Cusco, while Chuck and his Dad were taxiing out for takeoff in their plane, the Commandante of the airport called them back through the tower. They had previously met with the Commandante. Chuck was told that the Commandante wanted to speak with them.

After taxiing back, they met with the Commandante. The Commandante asked Chuck whether his Twin Comanche had normally aspirated engines. Chuck replied in the affirmative. The Commandante then said that he wouldn't advise their trying to fly out over the mountains in their plane to Cusco and landing in that city, which sits at an elevation of over 13,000 feet.

Chuck's reaction was that if the local Commandante of the airport went to all the trouble to call him back to the tower, his advice was worth listening to. Chuck eliminated Cusco from his flight plan. They took off and were flying along the coastal waters at 1,000 to 1,500 feet over the ocean.

Suddenly Chuck noted that there was no reflection coming up from the water and he became concerned. It was only after further investigation that he recognized that the cormorants were so thick over the ocean that there was no reflection. Bird guano is a major industry in north coastal Peru!

At about the same time, Chuck recognized that they were heading into a violent line squall. Knowing they had lifejackets and a lifeboat in the plane, Chuck decided to fly 75 miles out to sea to get around the squall. He couldn't make it to Antofagasta because of the detour out to sea.

So what did he do? He ended up radioing Arequipa and diverting into the mountains to Arequipa. Only problem was that Arequipa sits at an elevation of 11,000 feet, so they didn't lower their destination's elevation by much!

They didn't have to worry much about the length of the runway, because it was 2½ miles long because of the altitude.

While they were diverting, it was getting pretty late at night. Chuck called the tower to be sure that they would still be open. The controller indicated that normally they'd be closing, but he would wait for them. Chuck then asked him over the radio if there was any place where they could stay. The controller indicated that he would work on it.

When they got there, Chuck and his Dad experienced another example of warm and friendly Latin American hospitality.

The fellow was waiting for them out on the runway after they landed. He insisted on taking them out to dinner and also on a tour of *his* town. Chuck stated that the guy was very proud of his city and took them through structures like the city's historic Catholic chapel built in 1540.

After the royal treatment they had received, Chuck asked the gentleman if there was anything that he could get for him. The response was that he liked American cigarettes and American recordings. Chuck proceeded to purchase between 15 and 20 cartons of cigarettes and a dozen and a half records for his benefactor.

Chuck had a new Latin friend. Chuck and this gentleman remained in friendly communication for some 15 years after that evening.

From Chile, they next flew to central Argentina, heading towards Buenos Aires. They again encountered heavy weather and had to divert to Junin, Argentina. They landed on a grass field there.

Once again they were greeted by wonderful Latin American hospitality. The town brewer and the town tax collector became their instant amigos and paid for everything at that stop over.

They then went on to Buenos Aires where they stayed for three days. This was right after the passing of Juan Peron. Chuck commented that he was amazed at the depth of love and adoration the Argentinians had for Peron and his wife, Evita.

While they were in Buenos Aires, Chuck decided to fly out to Iguasu Falls, which is the largest falls in the world. Think Niagara Falls on steroids! *[I visited the falls once and I can offer personal testimony that it is an incredible sight!]* The falls are located on the border of Brazil and Argentina.

Chuck, being Chuck, took the direct approach to the falls. They flew up the river into the face of the falls and then, while he was taking moving pictures of the approach, Chuck pulled back on the yoke and they flew up and over the top of the cascading waters.

———————

The next stop was at their destination in São Paulo. However, upon starting their approach to the airport, Chuck received word that the entire airport was socked in by weather. Since he was low on fuel and Chuck couldn't legally fly IFR, that caused a very immediate problem.

The airport tower, through the highly irregular use of their approach radar system, helped Chuck safely land. That led to a quick relationship with a chap who was the Commandante for the Tactical Air Command for Brazil. That led to all manner of unusual social and flying opportunities with this gentleman and his family, including flying around the iconic sites in Rio.

One interesting side note added by Chuck about this Commandante. At the time of their visit, Brazil was in a very unstable political state. The Commandante quietly disclosed to Chuck the very complicated aviation escape plan he had put in place for him and his family in the event the country totally imploded to communism.

———————

There's a lot more to this Latin America saga, but I'm afraid Mike Burner's son, our publisher, will be in danger of running out of printer's ink! Therefore we will limit the balance of the story to the route taken back to the US by the intrepid explorers.

After the convention ended, they headed north to the mouth of the Amazon, then French Guiana, Trinidad and Tobago, then out over the ocean until Chuck noticed oil coming out of one of the engine nacelles. Diverting back to British Guiana, where things were very politically unstable, they were met on the airport runway by four jeeps with machine guns trained on them and told to move to the far end of the airport, fix the problem and get out of there.

On to Trinidad, then over the island of Tobago to Barbados and the Canadian airline stewardess – oops, that's for a different story. Next to Antigua, the Virgin Islands and the Sapphire Bay Beach Club, swimming with dolphins in the altogether – oops, there we go again! On to Nassau and all of its islands, and finally Fort Lauderdale, back in the good old Continental US!

———————

Chuck shared with me a lot of other stories about his life.

They included what almost seems to be the obligatory (maybe about half of our group) difficult divorce from his first wife and the depression that followed, only to be followed by an intriguing narrative about how he met his wife Heather, and she initially told him to get lost!

Fortunately, with the help of Heather's grandfather, she was forced to rethink her attitude and they have had a wonderful marriage of now nearly 52 years since her grandfather managed to straighten out her initial negative reaction to Chuck. It's an amazing story, but it's too long for this biography.

From the standpoint of Chuck's career, when he was finishing up his tour in the military, he was approached by the brand-new Tri-City hospital. They asked him to join with one other anesthesiologist in setting up an Anesthesiology Department for the hospital. Chuck worked for 34 years in that capacity. The anesthesiology group grew from their 2 original to members to 17 by the time he retired. In Chuck's words: "Good Years!!"

———————

Chuck is the latest and a recent addition to the Tuesday Morning Gang. Tracey Stratton originally became acquainted with Chuck's daughter, Sylvia, through a Christian women's group, a couple of years ago. That led to Chuck and Heather meeting Tracey and Skip, and Skip inviting Chuck to our meetings.

We are very thankful to have a doctor added to our esteemed group. His addition has greatly assisted us in our massive effort to meet the politically correct diversity levels required by today's society.

We already had more than enough pilots and attorneys among our members. The addition of Dr. Lindsay added an important medical element to that diversity objective, as well as bringing the group a little class!

Before closing Chuck's story, it's time for me to share a little secret with you. A few weeks back when I was trying to encourage Chuck to start putting together his life story, I sent him Bobby Beathard's informal biography as an exemplar. Chuck acknowledged to me that, after reading about Bobby's life, he was so intimidated by all that Bobby had accomplished that he didn't think it was worthwhile starting to tell his own story. He felt that his life story just wouldn't measure up, compared with Bobby's amazing life.

Well Doc, I think I can safely state on behalf of the gang that in fact your life history has measured up. Your biography is pretty darn incredible in its own right!

- eleven -

Pat O'Connor

Just got off the phone with Pat. Last Saturday I had asked him to put together some biographical information that I could use to get started on his story. Pat promised me that although he was fairly busy over in Indian Wells at their second home, he would try to get it to me sometime later this week.

However, being the ever efficient and focused former general contractor that he is, Pat had a very detailed chronology emailed to my home in less than a day.

Some of the rest you guys could take lessons from Pat when it comes to providing information about your lives. In a few of your individual cases, your personal information must be so precious that for me to get at it, it's like attempting to extract teeth with a limp piece of spaghetti!

Pat's rapid and candid response to my request for information epitomizes what I've learned about Pat through our meetings together over the last dozen years. *[As an aside, as near as we can determine, Pat and I joined the Tuesday Morning Gang at about the same time, 12 years ago.]*

With Pat, what you see is what you get!

No watered-down, equivocal responses from our Pat. If you either ask for his opinion, or Pat volunteers one, you're going to get the straight, unvarnished, and unexpurgated truth!

Based upon my observations, Pat has never had a thought in his lifetime which he considered politically incorrect and not worthy of stating publicly.

That's why I love the guy!!

My personal experience around talented and successful general contractors is that it's a shared trait. The general contractors who I have met and employed (for an extremely short period of time, I might add), who mince words and never give you a straight answer, are to be avoided at all costs!

Whether you're talking about politics at the local or national level, Pat is well versed and particularly strongly opinionated. Like most of the other guys in our group, Pat is concerned about America traveling down the slippery slope which led to the fall of the Roman Empire, which this country seems to be bound and determined to emulate.

_____

Enough on Pat's enviable philosophical approach. Let's get on with his illustrious life history.

Pat was born in Los Angeles at the beginning of the Great Depression. Fortunately, with respect to Pat's entrepreneurial propensities, that dire beginning didn't adversely impact the balance of his life!

In 1937 Pat's family moved to Hermosa Beach.

Once again, we encounter the arrival of another of the notorious Hermosa Beach Gang!

From 1937 through 1938 Pat attended public elementary school in Hermosa Beach.

Then, from 1939 to 1943, Pat attended St. James elementary school in Redondo Beach. When I asked him why he stopped going to the public school in Hermosa Beach, he mumbled something about a disagreement with the public school relating to either his deportment or the educational opportunities the school offered. I'm not sure which.

At the beginning of World War II, Pat began surfing in Hermosa Beach. Sadly, the fellow that he bought his first surfboard from went into the military during World War II, immediately after Pat's board purchase, and was killed while serving in the U.S. Navy on board an aircraft carrier.

In 1943, when he probably was about a freshman at Redondo High, Pat broke his arm playing football. That injury qualified Pat for the Wounded Warrior, Athletic Division, of the Tuesday Morning Gang (TMG).

The last couple of years of WWII, Pat managed to absolutely surf his brains out at Hermosa Beach, the Palos Verdes Cove, and Malibu.

Pat claims that he set some kind of surfing record with Dale Velzy when they surfed for 62 consecutive summer days at Malibu. Pat and Dale had first hooked up when they were still in grammar school.

Pat remembers that particular summer as having continuously spectacular surf at Malibu. Not only that, but they got to surf with some of the finest surfers ever during that time, including Buzzy Trent, Matt Kivlin, Peter Cole and his brother, and Bob Simmons. Simmons was the first guy in the surfing industry to incorporate foam into the manufacturing of surfboards.

———

From 1943, until after World War II was over in 1947, Pat split his high school experience between Redondo High School and Villanova, a private Catholic boys' boarding school located in Ojai.

According to Pat, he was the oldest of six kids. When his mother was pregnant again and the kids were kind of overwhelming her, Pat's dad decided to send Pat to Villanova.

As Pat tells the story, his dad was old-school. After observing that Pat was arguably spending more time surfing then he was going to school, his dad determine the best anecdote was a boys' Catholic boarding school!

Does the ever-present conflict for Pat between choosing to go surfing or attending school ring any bells of familiarity with any of the rest of you guys . . . particularly Woody?!

———

While he was in high school, Pat became quite a high school swimming sprinter. In 1946, his best times at Redondo High School were 25.3 seconds in the 50-yard sprint, and 56.4 in the 100-yard competition. Sharing Pat's swimming times with you makes me feel extremely inadequate.

I was also a sprinter on my high school swim team. Hell, one year I even won the New Haven, Connecticut, sprint championship at 50 yards, at the Yale pool.

I was very comfortable looking back at my high school performances, until Pat gave me the figures for his sprint records.

Don't tell anyone, but if we had competed against each other in the 50yard sprint, he would have been out of the pool and taking a hot shower by the time I finally hit the finishing wall!!

Not only that, but Pat said there were tons of other very fast sprinters in the South Bay when he was going through high school. Even with his stellar times, he wasn't the fastest guy in the county. He related that there were a couple of high school swimmers who were faster than he was, who later played water polo at USC with Pat. One of them went on to the Olympics.

You think maybe the ever-present sunshine in Southern California made the local swimmers that much faster than we kids back in the dark and gloomy Connecticut winters?

Pat graduated from Redondo High School in 1947, and that Fall entered USC on a full-time basis.

Instead of swimming competitively at USC, he competed on the men's water polo team. When I asked him why, he alluded to not being particularly enthusiastic about the nearly Germanic obsession with regimentation and discipline required of USC's competitive swimmers!

Besides, water polo players are much more manly than the swimmers that just splash back and forth in the chlorine, without anybody even trying to drown them!

By 1946, at the tender age of 17, Pat was such an accomplished surfer that he, along with Dale Velzy and Barney Briggs, were the only surfers that year to be inducted into the Hermosa Beach Surfing Club.

Apparently this club was a pretty exclusive ensemble. According to Pat, each year the new admittees to the club were limited to three individuals.

―――――――

The same year that Pat entered USC, 1947, he began a 10-year run as a seasonal lifeguard (full-time for about 18 months, starting in 1954 after he was discharged from the Coast Guard) with the Los Angeles County lifeguards. His lifeguarding service extended until 1957.

While he worked as a lifeguard, Pat was quite the accomplished performer during various Taplan lifeguarding competitions. One year he won the half-mile sprint paddling competition among all of the LA County lifeguards. He also performed as a dory man, anchored paddling relay teams, all when he wasn't competing on the lifeguards' surf team.

On the lifeguard surf squad he was competing with his teammates Don Grannis, Leroy's brother, and Ward Baker.

To summarize, as Pat recalls that era, he surfed and paddled on a competitive basis all over Southern California.

One extraordinary fact that Pat shared with me was that over the years of his life guard service he competed on eight different lifeguard teams and his teams never lost in any of those competitions!

―――――――

In June, 1951, Pat graduated from USC with a degree in business administration.

It appears that Howard Bugbee wasn't the only member of our group who decided that he'd prefer defending America's shores over getting his backside shot up by masses of deranged Chinese and Korean soldiers on the Korean Peninsula.

Pat joined the Coast Guard Reserves in May 1951, and then was on active duty from later that year, through 1953. While serving with the Coast Guard, Pat split his time about two-thirds being at sea, and the other third on good old terra firma.

Every time there was an opportunity for him to be promoted, he was. When he was discharged, he had achieved the rank of first-class quartermaster.

From my personal experience as a naval officer, I can tell you that Pat's rate of advancement through the ranks during his short two-year stint in the Coast Guard was quite meteoric!!

Pat's duty stations while in the Coast Guard included working on a buoy tender, home ported in Long Beach.

While he was serving on the buoy tender, Pat ran into Howard Bugbee who was also serving at that time in the Coast Guard.

Pat and Howard had originally become acquaintances back at Redondo High where Howard attended some meetings of a high school group that they were both associated with.

At the time of their getting together again in the Coast Guard, Howard was also assigned to the buoy tender.

Pat related to me a Howard Bugbee Coast Guard story that I feel compelled to share with you.

The story involved an incident that occurred while they were both serving their country (well, upon reflection, having heard the story below, it actually sounds like Pat was serving his country a little harder than Howard!).

———

One day Howard came to Pat to request some sick leave. Howard contended that he had a severely injured back and was not fit for duty.

Hearing this sad tale, Pat, not being fully apprised of Howard's well-earned reputation in the Coast Guard, granted permission for Howard to take sick leave that day.

———

As an aside, Pat told me that Howard may have heard that Dale Velzy had been discharged from active duty because he had a bad back.

Pat had first-hand knowledge of Velzy's back injury because he was a factor in causing that injury.

According to Pat, they had been surfing together and Pat's board, which got loose on a rather large wave, hit Velzy's back.

When you're on the water surfing, getting hit by errant surfboards is part of the everyday drill. However, in this instance, apparently Pat came off a big wave and lost his board. The surfboard went down the wave and crashed into Velzy's back.

With today's ultralight surfboards, Velzy's injury probably would've been limited to a slight dent in his back where the nose of Pat's board impaled him.

Unfortunately that wasn't the situation on that particular day when Velzy was hit by Pat's board.

The explanation is pretty simple.

Pat's surfboard weighed 105 pounds when it went smashing into Velzy's back!!

———————

As Pat explained it to me, on the day that he granted Howard not fit for duty status, Pat himself was 24 hours on and 24 hours off-duty.

When Pat finished his shift that day, he decided to go surfing at the Palos Verdes Cove. I'm not familiar with the approach to the beach, but according to Pat it's a very strenuous physical climb down to that revered surfing spot. Basically, you're clamoring down a cliff face.

After struggling down the rocky precipice to reach the beach, Pat climbed on his surfboard and paddled out.

Guess who he found on the outside, catching the biggest waves? None other than our beloved Howard, he of the severely disabled back!

Now most military people, particularly when they discover their hands firmly trapped in the cookie jar, display a serious state of contrition.

On that occasion, however, our Howard came up lacking a little in that department.

When he saw Pat come out and join him at the outside break, his immediate greeting was: "What took you so long to get here!?!"

———————

According to Pat, later on Howard did get official permission to spend some time away from his normal Coast Guard duties.

That was because he was training as a sprinter for the Olympics back in Annapolis, Maryland!!

After Pat was honorably discharged from the Coast Guard, he continued with some of his lifeguard work until, in 1955, a friend of his helped him get a construction job with Disneyland.

Prior to getting the Disneyland job, Pat built his first house in 1954 when he was only 25 years old.

While he was working at Disney, Pat started off as a gofer but was quickly promoted to more serious endeavors. Pat mentioned that he had some terrific mentors at Disney who worked with him on developing his construction skills.

In 1959, after working for Disney for a few years, Pat made a serious launch into his career as a builder.

Pat related that he built about 80 homes in Newport Beach, and 10 more between Laguna Beach and Capistrano. He also built 22 more homes in Costa Mesa.

Those included 16 waterfront homes in Newport Beach and Capistrano Beach, with the majority of them being in Newport.

In many of his projects, Pat offered design/build construction services. In other words, he pretty much handled everything from the original design of the home, the governmental permitting, building the structure, all the way to obtaining the certificate of occupancy for the new homeowner.

Pat indicated that the reason that he and his wife are comfortably retired at this juncture is that he also acquired and constructed some investment properties.

His investment properties included a large industrial building which he constructed for the O'Connor Brothers Abalone Co. The abalone company was a partnership with two of Pat's brothers.

———————

There's an interesting back story about the O'Connor Brothers Abalone Company.

In 1962/63, Pat built the large abalone processing plant and, upon the completion of the facility, he owned it.

The O'Connor Brothers operated the abalone processing plant for about four years here in California. Then, as all of us who used to love to eat abalone learned to our great chagrin, the California Fish and Game Department started giving out signals that it was going to severely cut back the local abalone take.

When Pat and his brother Mike recognized the adverse impact that Fish and Game was going to have on their abalone processing plant, they began contemplating relocating their operations.

Not being ones to pursue a restricted vision of that process, Pat and Mike decided to go global much before that became fashionable among American businessmen.

They decided to build and operate an abalone processing plant on the island state of Tasmania, Australia!

Tasmania is an island situated about 150 miles south of the Australian mainland. According to Pat, it's also a straight shot of about 800 miles to Antarctica!

———————

Pat shared an interesting tidbit about financing the construction of the Tasmanian abalone processing plant.

Once they had settled on a location for the proposed plant, Pat and his brother Mike talked to representatives of the Australian government concerning Australia making a construction loan for the project.

When the O'Connor brothers explained to the representatives that they would be employing about 20 local individuals in the processing plant, the Australian government, eager to create local jobs, agreed to make the construction loan.

———

In 1967 Pat made two visits to Tasmania; the first for two months and the second for seven months. He was in charge of building the new O'Connor Brothers' abalone processing plant on that island. His brother Mike was in charge of the plant's operations.

Pat was not only involved in the demands of constructing the new facility, but also ended up fighting the largest bush fire that has ever occurred in Tasmanian recorded history.

As Pat recalls it, on a Sunday there was a report of a large bush fire in the interior of the island. Once these fires get going, because of the prevalence of Gumtree forests (think eucalyptus trees), the bush fires have a tendency to burn like crazy.

Pat became concerned about the status of fighting the fire. He decided to talk about those efforts with the owner of the facility where he was staying. He indicated that the fellow was rather dismissive in his attitude about the fire, because he said it would rain and the rain would put the fire out.

Ultimately the local was correct in his assessment, but his

timing was off! According to Pat, the next day the wind really started blowing hard. Since, as I noted earlier, it is an 800-mile straight shot across the ocean to Antarctica, the storm winds on Tasmania are pretty fierce once they get going.

With the dry conditions and the fact that the gum trees ignite like matchsticks once the fire hits them, the fire was quickly out of control and threatening even downtown Hobart, the capital of Tasmania (present population a little over a half million).

Pat decided to go out and try to help fight the fire. However, the only firefighting equipment they had was wet sacks! Picture yourself in Southern California, with wet sacks, trying to beat back a huge fire coming at you through eucalyptus trees, driven by Santa Ana winds, and you kind of get the picture of what Pat was up against.

According to Pat, by the early evening it got pretty scary.

However, ultimately the wind shifted and then, as originally predicted by the local innkeeper, the rains finally came and knocked down the fire before it could reach the center of the capital, Hobart.

———

When they first began operating the abalone processing plant in Tasmania, the O'Connors were sending product back to the US on board ships. However, they quickly discovered that it was inefficient and costly, so they began to fly the abalone products back to the States.

Fortunately, after about four years of operating, they were approached by representatives of the Nissho Fish Company, the biggest of the Japanese fish companies.

They made a proposal that the O'Connor Brothers quickly

accepted. It involved shipping all of their product exclusively to Nissho, for consumption in Japan.

They streamlined the delivery process to ensure they would be going to market in Japan with fresh product. They affected this by delivering 50-pound containers of abalone products by air to the Tokyo fish market, within 24 hours of being shipped from Tasmania.

Eventually the Nissho Company made a proposal to buy the entire O'Connor Brothers processing plant in Tasmania, and Pat and Mike agreed to sell the complete operation to the Japanese.

With respect to the abalone processing plant that Pat had built and owned in Southern California, he leased the facility to various companies over a period of time until he finally sold it around the time when he moved to Cardiff, in 1976.

Pat also built an apartment house in 1972 as a personal investment. He still owns that apartment complex some 45 years later!

He had an interesting story about the original construction of that building.

By late 1972, Pat had obtained all of the local discretionary and building permits for the construction of the apartment complex.

The California Coastal Act had been approved by the California voters in 1972, and the California Coastal Commission became operative at the beginning of 1973.

In early 1973, with knowledge that his planned apartment building was within the California Coastal Commission's jurisdiction, Pat attempted to do the right thing by dealing with the Coastal Commission before he started construction.

The first time he went to the Commission's headquarters, he was told that the staff was out to lunch and wouldn't be back for a considerable period of time. *[As an aside, having had many encounters with the Coastal Commission staff as a land-use attorney during my legal career, it was my considered opinion that, figuratively speaking, the damn Coastal Commission staff was always out to lunch!!]*

In any event, Pat continued to try to do the right thing and ended up coming back two more times to the Commission headquarters in a vain effort to meet with staff.

When, for the third time, Pat was advised that the entire staff was off premises at a meeting or still out to lunch, the famous O'Connor temper finally took full control of the situation.

Pat went storming back to his project and built it! By the time the Coastal Commission finally discovered Pat's unpardonable transgression of building the structure without their approval, Pat already had the certificate of occupancy from the Newport Beach government and was filling the building with tenants!

Once again, my kind of guy!

The Coastal Commission and its staff were enraged by Pat's obvious flaunting of their vaunted authority. As a matter of fact, one of the Coastal Commission members, who was, in Pat's opinion, a total horse's backside, was particularly off the rails about the situation. Pat related that this individual had the memory of an elephant and never forgot what he did.

However, try as they might, at least on this occasion, the Coastal Commission and its bloody staff were totally stymied by Pat.

From the legal standpoint, the reason was pretty simple. Pat had all of his construction entitlements before the Coastal Commission jurisdiction came into operative legal effect.

Pat finished the story by mentioning that a doctor, who was constructing a commercial building, tried the same approach as the one adopted by Pat. Sadly, this guy got crushed by the Commission because, unlike Pat, he did not have his local entitlements in place before the Commission's jurisdiction became operative.

———————

Pat was also involved in building some commercial buildings for clients.

Those included the Bay and Beach Real Estate Building in Newport, which was a very large structure. Pat stated that his successfully completing that project got him a number of other major commercial property construction jobs.

Other buildings for clients included the three-story Harbor Inn, and a medical building, in Newport.

———————

As a contractor, particularly one constructing oceanfront buildings, Pat had his share of wild and hairy experiences.

Pat offered me one example.

He was building an oceanfront home in Newport Beach, at a time before the storm surf-reducing protective groins had been constructed along the beaches in that city.

Pat's crew had just inserted treated poles and begun other aspects of the construction of the foundation.

Suddenly, Pat was faced with an emergency. High tides and

large storm waves were predicted, which Pat accurately anticipated would devastate his construction site on the oceanfront.

Quickly adorning himself in his Captain Marvel contractor uniform, Pat raced to save his construction site from oceanic oblivion.

First he lined up the acquisition and transportation, through multiple dump trucks, of large amounts of sand to be delivered at the construction site.

Then he somehow managed to round up around a dozen college students from a couple of the junior colleges in the area. Those kids worked their fannies off bagging the sand and creating a temporary revetment to stave off the onrushing ocean.

Once again Captain (Pat) Marvel prevailed and saved the day for his client's project!

———

In 1976, Pat moved to San Diego and began to build homes. Many of the homes that he built in Encinitas and Vista were pole buildings.

Pat never lost touch with his surfing roots. As a matter of fact, whether he was building in Orange County, or later, here in San Diego, the nucleus of his workforce, the key guys, were always surfers.

For the record, a standard Pat O'Connor Construction Company work week with his construction crews was 4 days/week, 10 hours per day.

Adhering to this schedule, every weekend was a three-day weekend, which were always reserved for surfing!

———

Pat joined most of the rest of our gang in employing the trial and error approach to his early runs at matrimony.

Fortunately, as has also been the case with many of his brethren within our group, he finally got it right when, after four years of dating, he married Viola.

Twenty-eight years later, together they are enjoying Pat's personal best performance when it comes to matrimonial longevity!

Pat related that he has two daughters and one son. He then lamented that for more years than he wants to count, he hasn't had a relationship with his son.

I commented to Pat that once again this seems to be a common theme running through many of the members of our gang, including me. It seems like a number of us have a rocky, or no relationship, with one of our children.

After cogitating about it for a considerable period of time, the only explanation that made any sense to me was this.

Our common problem of having a difficult relationship with one of our kids has to be traced back to the contents of John's coffee that he serves to our gang at the Seaside Market!

———————

Since I first came up with the idea of gathering together the biographies of the Tuesday Morning Gang, I have waited with great anticipation for the opportunity to put together Pat O'Connor's story.

There's a reason I felt that way. Pat is a very quiet and reserved individual. (That's at least the case if he's not talking about politics!) After being around him for a number of years, I found him to be a very bright and interesting guy who, by the comments that he drops every once in a while, clearly has lived a rather extraordinary life.

And you know what? My excited anticipation was not disappointed once he did reveal his life story to me.

Pat O'Connor has lived one hell of an interesting life!!

- twelve -

Havasu Bill a.k.a. Yuma Bill Taggart

Mister Taggart is sort of the wayward son of the Tuesday Morning Gang.

When I first joined the group about 12 years ago, Bill's attendance at our meetings was exemplary. That was during the period when he lived on the coast. However, when he was transformed into "Yuma Bill," living on a ranch in Yuma, Arizona, the multi-hour commute to and from Cardiff in order to attend our hour and a half meetings, wasn't insurmountable, but was definitely a bit of a challenge.

Of course that didn't always deter our diehard Bill, who still managed to make it to some meetings in spite of the vicissitudes of his interstate commute.

I'll mention Bill's second divorce later in this piece, but after that had been initiated, he moved to Lake Havasu, California. This move meant that he didn't have to become involved in interstate commerce in order to attend our meetings. However, that's still a pretty long hike in a car when the objective is to sit and listen to a bunch of old duffers lying to each other about what they did when they were not of such advanced years.

But we're getting ahead of ourselves. Let's go back to Bill's earlier days, BTMG (Before Tuesday Morning Gang).

Bill was born on August 1, 1946, in Astabula, Ohio. His father had just got out of the Air Force (bombardier/navigator in the Pacific Theater of World War II). In writing a quick note to me about his biography, Bill used the phrase quoted above, "just got out of the Air Force."

[Since my mind has a tendency to wander during the preparation of these biographical narratives, I had to wonder about the accuracy of those words. Whether there was a correlation between his dad being mustered out of the Air Force and Bill's arrival, probably about nine months later. Somehow I think there may be such a connection. In any event, the timing was noteworthy because Bill now enjoys the notoriety of being one of the original pioneers of the Baby Boomer generation!]

Anyway, the family moved to California and Bill's dad was hired by a radio station in Sacramento. Initially he was an engineer and later he had his own radio show called *Unit 99* (Bill: think the TV show *COPS*, but his dad narrated the program on the radio).

Do you think that maybe his dad's radio show had a later influence on Bill's career path decisions?

Subsequently, when his dad began working on computers, the family moved to Torrance. That move added another member to the ubiquitous and notorious South Bay Gang that the rest of us have to deal with every Tuesday morning!

After Bill arrived in Torrance, it wasn't long before he initially hooked up with the other member of the Fearless Twosome, Jim

Thompson. From that point on they became BFFs. *[I have no idea what these initials stand for, but since my grandchildren use them rather freely in referring to their "besties," I have to assume the translation is not R-rated.]*

Jim and Bill subsequently went to high school and law school together. Not only that, but Bill relates that each of them served as the best man for the other, not only for one marriage ceremony, but for a second one as well, since both of them divorced and remarried.

When I learned that Jim appeared in Bill's life at such an early stage, a fiendish thought struck me.

Every time these two guys get together at our meetings, and even sometimes when Jim is there without Bill, we hear another fabulous tale of the globetrotting antics of these two characters.

The thought I had was, instead of my trying to lamely cobble together their erratic life journeys, why don't we have Bill prepare Jim's biography, and Jim reciprocate by telling Bill's story. If we proceed in that manner, we may get a hell of a lot more candor about their respective illustrious lives. As a matter of fact, if their stories are told in that fashion, we might end up hearing some real nitty-gritty, down and dirty stuff!

At age 11 or 12, Bill and Jim started surfing together. One summer later, Bill reports that the first *Gidget* movie came out in theaters and screwed up their surfing adventures. The reason was the massive surfing crowds that followed the arrival of that movie. As reported by Bill, instead of having 7 other surfers out there with them at their favorite break, the number had skied all the way up to 10!

While attending Torrance high school, Bill and Jim had a wonderful time playing football together.

And in the category of it's a small world, in the summer following Bill's Junior year in high school, he and a friend worked for Bobby Beathard's dad at his tile plant in El Segundo. The following summer, he worked there again for a few months.

When Bill graduated from high school, Uncle Sam came calling. He received his draft notice in 1966 and enlisted for flight training. Unfortunately, Bill was unable to follow in his dad's aviation footsteps because he failed an eye examine and was disqualified from flying.

Following the disqualification, Bill had an examination by a civilian optometrist who confirmed he had substandard vision. However, the optometrist stated that his eyesight was off by such a small margin that if the atmospheric conditions on that day had been different, he would've passed the eye test.

At this juncture, Yuma Bill and the U.S. Army had different visions of Bill's future military career. When Bill advised the army of the results of the civilian optometrist eye testing and requested a retest, the Army apparently pulled a bait and switch.

Bill was told that if he joined the Army as a medic, in six months they would waive the eyesight disqualification and he would be sent on to flight training.

For some reason, subsequently, apparently the Army personnel office got a little confused cutting his new orders. After Bill had been trained as a medic, instead of being sent to flight training, as promised, our Bill ended up as a medic in Vietnam during 1966-1967!

Bill's reaction to this little game of military legerdemain pulled by the Army: "My naïveté astounds me!"

[Editor's aside: Bill has got to have a bunch of Vietnam stories that he can share with us.]

After his discharge from the Army, Bill attended El Camino Junior College. While going to college, he obtained financial sustenance from a variety of different jobs.

He was an ambulance driver and attendant, a taxi driver in Hermosa Beach (any of you guys remember the blue-and-white cabs?), managed a pool hall, and taught preschool (sporting a provisional credential, whatever that means) for one summer.

Then, since he had so much spare time, he began racing motocross motorcycles!

Bill was having a great time with his motorcycle racing except for one thing. As you start winning, they keep moving you up in class and pretty soon he found himself in a Pro class.

In Bill's words: "That was the end of winning."

Bill's lame excuse for not be able to win as a pro was something along the following lines.

Just because he had to borrow money to buy gas so that he could make it to the start line on his motorcycle, he thought the competitions were a little unfair.

He came to that wimpy conclusion based on the fact that most of the guys who were at the start line with him at these Pro motocross competitions had arrived with professional mechanics who didn't speak any English, and were supported by a 40-foot trailer that had an inexhaustible supply of motorcycle parts.

However, what was really galling for Havasu Bill was the fact

THE TUESDAY MORNING GANG ANTHOLOGY

that each of these tricked-out professional motocross riders had been a pro for at least 10 years and were considerably younger than he was!

But the saving grace for Bill was that he had such a strong fan base to support his motocross aspirations.

Of course his fan base was solely comprised of Jim Thompson. However the important thing was that Jim was extremely enthusiastic rooting for Bill while he was on the track during his races.

As an example, on one occasion when Bill was racing at Ascot Park in Gardena, Jim got so carried away rooting for Bill that when Bill, who was leading for the first time, rounded a corner during the competition, he was suddenly confronted by Jim running out onto the track waving, yelling, and urging his BFF on!

For some unknown reason, the race officials took umbrage at Jim's spirited support of his buddy.

———

Despite the fact that he was racing three times a week, lacking any sponsorship backing, eventually Bill recognized that Jim's exuberant fan support alone was not going to be sufficient to earn him a living at motocross racing.

Having come to that conclusion, Yuma Bill finally hung up his helmet, shin guards, and the other protective devices one wears when one is bound and determined to test the tensile strength of one's body's bone structure on such a frequent basis.

———

About this time, the apple didn't fall that far from the tree. Bill picked up on his dad's old radio show and joined the LA Sheriff's Department.

As a County Sheriff, Bill spent 15 years chasing the bad guys. His duties included custody, the Bail Bureau, patrol out of the Lennox station, field training officer, and as a detective working on robberies.

While he was a Sheriff, the Fearsome Twosome got together again and attended law school at night.

Following law school, in Havasu Bill's words: "Jim passed the bar on his first attempt and I did not."

At that time, Bill left the Sheriff's Department and transferred to the Public Defender's office, as an investigator. He retired 11 years later as a branch supervisor.

[Author's note: Between 15 years in the Sheriff's Department and 11 years as an investigator for the Public Defender, I have the feeling that Yuma Bill is withholding an incredible number of terrific stories from his Tuesday Morning friends! Maybe his bestie, Mister Thompson can help us out here.]

During his years with the Sheriff's and Public Defenders offices, Bill solidified his South Bay, Hermosa Beach creds, by owning a home in that fair city at 136 2nd Street.

[Once again I have a sneaking suspicion that there may be a hidden cache of stories related to that home ownership in that locale!]

———

Yuma Bill temporarily bailed on his Hermosa Beach connections by selling his home and buying a home in Huntington Harbor when he was 40 years old. His flimsy rationale for making that traitorous transfer of home ownership was that the new home had a boat dock that would hold his 37-foot Striker Sport Fisher.

He met his first wife following that move. He married her five years later, and it only took three more years before they got a divorce.

According to Bill, he put his wife through optometry school and, upon completion, they opened three optometry practices. Furthermore, as Bill related, "when the income got good, she did not need me anymore and we divorced."

One year before the divorce, they had moved from Huntington Harbor to Coto de Caza, in Orange County.

When they divorced, Bill sold the Orange County home, as well as his Defever Trawler.

———————

Being the man of action that he is, when Havasu Bill retired, he moved to Fort Lauderdale, Florida, and bought a really big sailboat, 80 feet long! *[Editor's note: as I recall, there is one hell of a back story about the purchase of that sailboat that Bill is holding out from his Tuesday Morning friends! Once again, I'm sure Jim Thompson can help out here.]*

One would normally expect that that type of precipitous bi-coastal move would've cut Bill's ties to Southern California. Not so.

The reason was that his BFF came back into his life again.

The basis for their getting back together in Florida was this.

Yuma Bill had always had boats and was quite familiar with boat handling, marine navigation, and the like. However, this was the first time that he purchased a sailboat. Since Jim Thompson had owned sailboats, it was natural for Bill to contact his BFF for assistance.

Ever ready for adventure, particularly with his wayward

friend Bill, Jim, his wife Anita, and their two kids, flew down to Florida, to crew on this mighty vessel.

———————

Havasu Bill and his merry crew sailed the Bahamas for a few weeks. Bill relates that they had one regular crew member during the trip. The guy was not a particular pleasure to be around. As Bill saw him, he was: "The one crew member who had the distinction of being the only person I knew who was immediately hated by everyone who met him (Jim almost beat him up). Kept him aboard so I could learn tolerance."

When they finally reached the Panama Canal, they threw the despicable S.O.B. overboard.

In reviewing Bill's notes about his life, I was somewhat surprised to see that his narration relative to this particular maritime adventure ended at this point. I knew something was missing because the BFFs have told us that there was a heck of a lot more to this seafaring saga, including wrecking the boat at some point.

Oh well, just another hole in Bill's life narrative which will need to be filled in by Jim at some later time.

———————

After they finally arrived back in San Diego, Bill stayed for over 20 years.

He had been in San Diego for about a month when he met his second wife to be. In 1998, they bought a horse ranch together in Jamul (Bill refers to that little town as "The all Caucasian ghetto").

He and his new wife had a happy coexistence in Jamul ". . . until my wife descended into drug addiction."

Then they did what was referred to during my first wife's alcoholic years, as a "geographic." That means you move to a new area with the hopes that the addiction demons will continue to reside where you used to live and not move to your new abode.

To put it in Bill's words: "Hoping a change of environment would be beneficial (two failed rehabs), we moved to Yuma, Arizona."

Thus Bill managed to earn his first sobriquet: "Yuma Bill."

Sadly, things didn't work out for them after the move. "Two years later I concluded that she had no intentions for sobriety and had her removed from the home, sold it and moved to Lake Havasu, Az."

Thus earning his second a.k.a. of "Havasu Bill"!

[I've been joking a little bit about what Bill went through with his wife's addictions. Having spent about a decade of my own life following a similar marital path, I'm here to share with you that those segments of one's life leave you with some rather massive emotional scarring. Occasionally Bill has shared with us some of the craziness that has occurred over the last year and a half since he separated from his wife. Sadly the divorce is still dragging on.]

I sent my original draft of this material to Bill to get his feedback.

In his response, he said some nice things about the effort going into this project.

Bill also stated, rather emphatically, that he had absolutely no interest in granting a license to Jim Thompson to present his version of Yuma Bill's biography! His extremely lame excuse for putting the kibosh on that concept was:

"I am hesitant to have Jim expose me as I am apprehensive about the statute having run."

In any event, with my editorial urging, fortunately Havasu Bill came up with an additional saga involving his adventures on the high seas.

That story, among his seemingly endless maritime escapades, follows.

————————

A couple of months after they initially got together in San Diego, Janell and Bill decided to take their ginormous sailboat down to the Sea of Cortes for the winter.

On the trip they anticipated that they would be blessed with fabulous dining. An acquaintance accompanied them on the trip who was a Cordon Bleu trained chef. The agreement was that he would also stand watches.

As related by Bill, they left San Diego on a Tuesday and their gourmet chef immediately retreated to his cabin because he was extremely seasick.

The chef's condition did not improve in any way during the 500-mile trip to Turtle Bay. They finally reached the harbor of Turtle Bay, after that extremely long sail, at midnight on Saturday. During those days, they had to scrounge up their own meals, and the master chef wasn't even available to stand any watches.

When they arrived outside the harbor, according to Bill, since he didn't get any piloting relief, he hadn't slept since the previous Wednesday, three days earlier.

————————

At this juncture, in what Bill had originally envisioned as a dream sailing trip, the fun and games really began.

When he arrived off the Turtle Bay Harbor, Janell was asleep.

Because he does not enter an unfamiliar harbor at night, and they were 15 miles offshore with no wind or waves, Bill made the command decision to drift until sunrise.

Wrong!

After collapsing into his bunk, totally exhausted, Bill was rudely awakened by multiple loud banging noises and crashing sounds.

Because he was not aware of a strong current that ran in that locale, intensified by Cedros Island, Captain Courageous, a.k.a. Yuma Bill Taggart, had managed to run his gigantic sailboat aground.

Somehow Bill was able to separate his boat from the rocks that had accosted his mighty ship in such a stealthy manner, and began inspecting his vessel for the expected damage.

Since, from the nautical standpoint, the description of the damage is highly technical, and furthermore since I spent 4-½ years on active duty in the Navy, but never set foot on a naval vessel that was actually underway, I will have to defer to Havasu Bill's description of his maritime survey of his damaged cruise ship.

"Upon entering the engine room, the floor boards were awash. I had six 12 V bilge pumps and two 24 V pumps with 1 ½ inch pipes. The hull damage was so extensive the pumps were overcome by the volume of entering water. The main engine and two generators were hard plumbed so I was unable to use their raw

water intake lines as pumps. The engine room was one
of seven water-tight compartments and I could only
dog the water-tight door as it flooded."

*[Jim, can you please translate what the hell Bill said and put it
in plain English for we landlubbers!]*

In answer to Bill's emergency radio call, a large motor yacht
towed the boat into Turtle Bay where Bill anchored. Bill tried to
offer reasonable compensation to the owner of the motor yacht,
but the gentleman graciously declined. Little did they know that
their maritime Good Samaritan was in reality, a rapacious Pirate.

More on that later.

———————————

After they were finally towed into the harbor, Bill and Janell
stayed in town for seven days while they awaited the arrival of
the salvage crew that would be taking charge of their boat.

During their stay in the little village, Bill stated that they
were never pan handled nor did they ever feel threatened by
anyone. Generally the reception was very cordial.

Because of their anticipated long stay in the Sea of Cortes,
Bill had several thousand dollars worth of provisions on board
the vessel, a large portion of which was frozen.

Since there was no power on the Yuma Bill yacht, our Bill
engaged in a very significant act of charity. He distributed all of
the free food around the town to the impoverished people!

He also had about 1,800 gallons of fuel on his boat to
dispose of. Since there was a shrimp fleet anchored in the Turtle
Bay Harbor, he sold the fuel to members of the fleet at 50% of
the actual value.

He and Janell then spent the next five or six weeks hitch hiking and taking buses around Mexico.

When they finally returned to the good old US of A, with less than 10 pesos in Bill's pocket, they were met by further bad news. As if the Fickle Finger of Fate had not messed with them enough, they were suddenly confronted with the true nature of the "Good Samaritan" who had towed them into the harbor.

Captain Rapacious had filed a salvage claim against Bill's boat! Not only that, but he asserted in the claim that his reasonable compensation for his "heroic rescue actions" entitled him to the title to Bill's boat!

Under the laws of the sea, seamen who rescue stricken vessels can file certain monetary claims for reasonable compensation.

Sounds like this guy was a nefarious pro at twisting the laws of the sea to suit his own voracious appetite for money and assets.

His claim alleged that he exposed his vessel and crew to extreme danger from high winds, large waves, and a lee shore, in towing Bill's sailboat into the harbor.

The Admiralty Courts look at weather conditions and all potential hazards to the rescuing vessel and its crew in calculating any award that is made.

As Bill tells the story, in order to support his maritime claim, Captain Rapacious submitted a photograph of himself standing against his transom, with Bill's stricken boat in the background.

According to Bill:

> "The photo was large, of excellent quality, sharply in focus, depicting great detail; bright sunshine, the calm flat sea and that towline slack and curvy on the water."

Sounds like the Admiralty Court was onto this clown's shenanigans. As reported by Bill, the idiot's award by the court was for reasonable towing compensation of approximately $1,000.

Sadly for the self-proclaimed maritime hero, previous to receiving the award, he had brazenly passed on a story to the *Log* (a bi-monthly newspaper for the boating community) setting forth in great detail his bravery and heroism in the rescue of Yuma Bill's vessel and crew that was doomed if it hadn't been for his actions!

Sometimes, but unfortunately not often enough, karma comes around and bites bad folks on the backside!

———————

Bill has written his own epilogue to this brief biographical sketch.

"I have been staying busy with boating on the river, working on some cars, driving my Dune buggy and searching for women with a grandfather fetish. I do miss surfing and my friends."

- thirteen -
Jim Thompsen

Having just finished Roy Bream's story, I thought I had been exposed to the ultimate Career Course Correction Champion (CCCC) among the members of our group. However, after having finished looking through Jim Thompsen's notes about his life, I can see that he and Roy are pretty much neck and neck in that department!

Jim was born in December 1946, in Los Angeles, a little over a year after the end of World War II.

Due to forces completely beyond Jim's control, Jim's younger life was quite nomadic.

For the first three years, he lived in various parts of the San Fernando Valley. His granddad owned 10 acres and a feed store in the Valley at the corner of Victory and Van Owen.

Jim's next entry is somewhat intriguing. It's to the effect that he "was kidnapped by my father (marital dispute between mom and dad) and was whisked away to San Marcos where my aunt operated a dairy farm."

He goes on to state that in 1951 he started school at 4½ years of age in San Marcos, in a one room schoolhouse.

Then his chronology, without so much as a word of explanation, indicates that he was returned to Hollywood to his great-grand-mother who had owned her home there since the 1920s.

And here comes the South Bay connection!

Jim then moved to Torrance "in the latter part of 1952 or early '53, can't be sure of the exact date as CSR is setting in." *[Editor's note: Since I wasn't familiar with that acronym, I Googled "CSR." I found that it related to either Corporate Social Responsibility or a Certificate Signing Request. Taking a wild-ass guess at it, I think Jim was probably talking about a Senior Moment. Jim has now confirmed that. He says it should have read CRS, meaning "Can't Remember (Stuff)."]*

The next event in Jim's life was momentous. He met Bill Taggart (a.k.a. Yuma Bill or Havasu Bill) in the 5th grade at Carl Steele Elementary School. And thus we witness the initial formation of the Fearsome Twosome!

———

At my prompting, Jim shared with me some stories about the young adventures of the Fearsome Twosome, as well as escapades after they became adults (and I have to acknowledge that I use the descriptive word "adults," advisedly!).

The first story involved these two characters when they were only 11 or 12 years old. Along with a couple of buddies, they rode their single-speed Schwinn bicycles from Torrance, on Artesia Boulevard (before it was a major roadway), 35 miles to Knotts Berry Farm and back in a single day.

> "None of our parents knew of the adventure before it happened. Needless to say, we all got back way after dark and all hell broke loose!"

The next story occurred when the Dynamic Duo were about 13 or 14.

"We went to our friend's house to shoot peas through our pea shooters. We each had a full bag of peas. Someone decided to get on the roof of Bob Hedrick's house (that would have been me) and Bob decided to get in a trash can along the curb. I think Bill was on the roof of the house and we all started to shoot peas at each other. This soon degenerated into shooting peas at passing cars. A fellow in a top-down convertible came by and we all started pelting the vehicle. The guy slams on his brakes and puts the car in reverse, backing into the trash can on the curb with Bob inside, flinging him out of the trash can, at which time he began running down the street with the irate motorists in pursuit. At this time Bill and I get off the roof and hightail it to my house a couple blocks away and hide until Bob calls us to tell us he outran the pursuing motorist."

The next story involves Yuma Bill racing his motorcycle.

"Bill was racing motocross at Ascot Park in Gardena. I was there with a couple of friends to support him in the pits. Bill was riding a Czech bike called a CZ360. Bill had changed out the Jekov carb for a Japanese Mikuni, more reliable he thought. Unfortunately, Bill removed the heatsink material from the Jekov, and when he installed the Mikuni there was no insulating material between the carb and the cylinder head. Big problem. When the cylinder unit heated up so did the carburetor, resulting in the carb material expanding and causing the throttle to stick. Not immediately, but usually about the second or third lap of the race. Guess what? The throttle stuck on the second lap, just as Bill was going into a turn. He went straight and flew off the track. He was knocked out. So, we loaded him and the bike into his van and went to Gardena Memorial Hospital. They checked him out and released him in about an hour. Bill says, I think I can make my next race, so back we go to Ascot. Bill does make the race, however, the bike does the same thing, but this time before the race starts. What luck. It wasn't until he talked to the CZ dealer in Redondo Beach that he realized what the problem was. The dealer said he did the carb exchange all the time, but you had to install a rubber insulator between the carb and the cylinder."

The next story involving the Intrepid Twosome occurred while they were diving for abalone.

"We're at Santa Barbara Island diving for abalone at Bill and Jim's secret spot. Bill had his limit of abs and decided to go spearfishing. He spots about 100 Rays on the bottom and takes a shot. Direct hit, however the Ray takes off and starts pulling Bill out of the cove into open water. I'm on the boat and I look out the stern and see Bill surface with his BC inflated and he is yelling at me to come get him. However, the Ray is still pulling Bill around like a buoy behind a speedboat. Finally, the Ray tires and Bill is able to pull it back to the boat stern. The Ray is still alive and has some life to it. Bill gets on the boat, we tied the line to a clete to keep the Ray, and Bill gets out of his diving gear. We then pull the Ray into the cockpit. It's huge. It starts flapping its wings and flailing its tail. Bill grabs a short bat and starts beating the flailing Ray. There is blood all over the deck and the Ray is still not dead. After about 10 minutes of this, the thing finally succumbs. We filleted the wings and took them home along with about 20 abs for dinner and freezing."

A couple more chapters in the fun-filled life of the Fearsome Twosome!

———————

Time to get back to Jim's high school years.

Jim initially started high school at North Torrance High. Then came a divorce between his mom and dad, and he moved with his dad to Manhattan Beach and transferred to Mira Costa High School.

Jim's chronology then makes reference to "Skip Stratton, Tommy Dunne, et al." I assumed this was shorthand for Jim getting to know some of the members of the South Bay Gang while attending Mira Costa High School. Seems like most of the South Bay contingent went to high school there at one time or another.

Jim did make a correction to my assumption. Actually, Skip

and Tommy Dunne graduated from Mira Costa a few years before he got there. He was making reference to the fact that many of our members went to Mira Costa.

Jim's dad remarried in 1963. Ever on the move, Jim lived in Torrance again for a short period of time, then moved to Hermosa Beach, and then once more, back to Torrance.

Has anybody been keeping track of the number of moves Jim made before he left for college? I had no idea that a youngster could possibly have to suffer through that many moves without his dad being in the armed services.

―――――――

With that kind of childhood, it's no wonder that Jim has spent the last few years constantly searching all over Florida for a new place to move to. Fortunately for Jim, I think he finally found the perfect fishing accessible spot for his retirement and has just closed escrow on a Florida lot!

―――――――

Jim reports that he played two years of varsity football at West Torrance High and, in Jim's words, "where I graduated, barely."

―――――――

Jim started surfing in 1958. He bought his first surf board from Dale Velzy. He and Havasu Bill started the Bay City Surf Club in approximately 1960, with six other surfing gremmies.

Pat Bonner was the oldest member of their surf club, and worked for Jim Lyman, Lyman Surfboards, as a shaper and glasser.

Yuma Bill and Jim were the youngest at about 14. At that

stage they had been surfing for a couple of years. Their trips ranged from Santa Cruz (one time) to Mexico.

Most of their trips headed North as far as Rincon, and there were a lot of Malibu trips thrown in. They also headed down to San Diego, with surfing stops in Laguna, San Clemente, and Dana Point before the harbor was built.

One memorable trip, they left Redondo Beach in Bonner's '56 Ford pick up, with a pony keg and his new board in the back which had just been glassed hours before with a "hot gloss coat."

Joining them in their surfing convoy was Ron Haslip in his '46 Woody, and a third vehicle that was a '59 El Camino crammed with surfboards.

They headed South for Salt Creek and Dana Point. Salt Creek was a state campground (way before the Four Seasons was built above it).

They got to their camp site and started surfing and drinking beer. They apparently got a little loud and rowdy, and the Rangers evicted them from the campsite about midnight. Of course you have to keep in mind that Bill Taggart and Jim were around 14 or 15 at that time and were probably surrounded by cups of beer!

They didn't know what to do next, so they went back to Laguna Beach and parked in a vacant lot next the old McDonald's on PCH.

Next morning they all got up early, "no cops!" and took off headed South to the Oceanside pier for another surf session.

Jim kept up his surfing until he entered military service in 1964 when he joined the Air Force. He was only 17 at the time.

I asked him what prompted him to go into the service. Was he concerned about the draft because of Vietnam heating up?

Jim's answer was in the negative. He had recently graduated from high school and couldn't get a decent job at the time because he needed to be 18. He went on to state that he wasn't interested in school then and was living with his grandmother in Hawthorne.

> "One day I'm driving down Torrance Boulevard, coming from the beach in my '58 Bug Eye Sprite. My buddy Moon Man (he was almost bald in HS) was with me and we ran out of gas. I had no money; he had just a little for a couple of gallons. We put gas in the car and said let's join the Air Force. He said let's join the Marines. I said they have to sleep on the ground in tents and have s....y food, my dad was in the AF and they have a roof over their heads, sleep on thick mattresses and have excellent food. So we headed to the recruiter in downtown Torrance and signed up. However, I had to get my mom's permission as I wasn't 18. She was happy to sign, that way she didn't have to support me any longer. That is a story for another day."

Jim went through basic training at Lackland Air Force Base in Texas. He then attended technical school in Amarillo, Texas. Jim was apparently a computer whiz because he completed an advanced computer school course scheduled for 10 weeks, in only 6 weeks!

Jim was next sent to SAC Command, 91st Bomb Wing, Glasgow, Montana. While stationed there he completed additional computer courses and took the Sergeant exam and passed it with a 95 percentile score!

That was one amazing feat! At the time he was just 18 years of age and by that point hadn't been in the Air Force for even a year. And he's already aced the Sergeant exam while he was still an Airman! For those of you who have read Pat O'Connor's life story, does the rapid advancement in military rank sound familiar?!

It appears that the Air Force quickly wised up to the kind of talent that they were blessed with in Jim. At this juncture he was offered an appointment to the Air Force Academy!

When that offer was made to him, Jim thought about it for a while and then realized that he wasn't sure that he liked the military all that much.

If he had accepted the appointment at the Air Force Academy, it would have amounted to a lengthy commitment. A nine-month prep school, then four years at the Air Force Academy, followed by a five-year commitment on active duty if he wanted to become a flyboy.

Having turned down the appointment to the Air Force Academy, Jim then did the only logical thing that he could given the circumstances. He volunteered to go to Vietnam!?!

The way Jim tells it, one day one of the sergeants in his unit came through the office and asked if anyone would be willing to take his assignment to Vietnam, as his daughter had been severely burned in a floor heater accident about a week or two before. She had been transported to Randolph Air Force Base for burn treatment and skin grafting. The Sergeant wanted to join her there. Jim asked the Sergeant:

> "Where in Vietnam? He replied Da Nang. I said is it warm. He replied Hell yes! I was in. I had to go through some counseling, they thought I was nuts, and get a dispensation. I had passed the Sergeant's exam but was only an Airman 2nd Class. Since I had the Sergeant's AFSC (Air Force Specialty Code), they allowed me to take the assignment."

The back story is that Jim was in Glasgow, Montana for 14 months. According to Jim, the place was cold all but six weeks of late spring and a brief summer. He was ready to go *anywhere* to get the heck out of the cold!

———————

Jim served at the Da Nang Air Force Base from July 1966 to July 1967. During that time he was promoted to Sergeant, while he was still only 19, after less than one year's time in grade as an Airman Second Class. As Jim put it, that promotion was "unheard of at that time."

Having spent some 7½ years of active and reserve duty with the U.S. Navy, I can attest that military promotions of this type just flat don't happen!

While serving in Da Nang, Jim was awarded the Air Force Commendation Medal for Vietnam service. Jim was told that his superiors had put him in for a Bronze Star, but the award was reduced.

I asked Jim what he did to earn the award. Jim's response, in his normal laconic style:

> "As far as my citation, I have no idea why I got it and others didn't. Maybe it was because I volunteered for a lot of (stuff) that others didn't. The citation accompanying the medal said a lot of good things that I did serving in country, but all of them say good things about the recipient. That's all I can say about that."

Against my better judgment, I was going to leave this rather cryptic explanation alone and overcome my intrepid journalistic inclination to pry further.

But of course Jim, being Jim, managed to somewhat clear up the matter, although I'm sure he didn't intend that result.

At our next Tuesday morning meeting, I overheard him talking with other members of our gang about serving in Da Nang with a lot more specificity than he had bothered to offer to me when I was trying to wrest information out of the guy. Not only that but he started talking about his experiences at Vietnam's version of Malibu surfing, China Beach.

Since I was talking with someone else at that moment I only picked up up bits and pieces of Jim's conversation. I'll do my best to reconstruct a little of the information.

First of all Jim was a real surfer at China Beach.

China Beach was set up by the military for in-country R&R purposes for the troops. The vast majority of troops that came out to the beach had been battling the Vietcong and North Vietnamese in the jungles. I'm sure a very low percentage of those individuals had ever surfed before in their lives.

According to Jim, these guys would come out for a couple of days of R&R and then get tossed back into the middle of the war. On the other hand, since Da Nang was right adjacent to China Beach, Jim was able to spend more time at the beach.

Having served his gremmie time and early surfing apprenticeship in the South Bay, Jim was a full-on surfer by the time he arrived on China Beach.

Before turning to my version of why Jim got a commendation awarded to him during his service in Da Nang, I want to share with you some information about China Beach today.

Obviously, at the time of the Vietnam War, the amenities were quite limited in the immediate area of the beach.

Researching the subject, I read an article by a guy who said he visited China Beach in the early 1980s and it had one resort at that time. However, at the time of his recent visit, it had 150 resorts with more on the way!

Doesn't seem possible. However, the information that I turned up during my investigation indicated that the beach itself is about 20 miles long and is absolutely gorgeous, by any beach resort standards.

––––––––

Since I don't expect to get any further details from the man himself, time to turn to my speculative version of the basis for Jim's award.

During the overheard conversation, Jim casually mentioned that during his one-year stay in Da Nang, the bad guys made at least three rocket attacks on the base where he was stationed. Not only that but apparently the Marines, who shared the base with the Air Force, suffered some severe casualties during those rocket attacks.

Specifically, I heard Jim make the offhand remark that he responded to one of the attacks by getting to a Marine shrapnel victim whose carotid artery had been cut. Jim just shook his head and said that he didn't believe how badly the young guy bled from the shrapnel wound.

Although I didn't hear Jim's statement about the ultimate outcome, it sounded to me as if the Marine didn't make it.

My guess is that the commendation award that almost became a Bronze Star, might have been related to Jim's activities during those enemy rocket attacks.

Correction: I ran this scenario by Jim this morning at our meeting and he indicated it was incorrect. The story about the wounded Marine is correct but that wasn't the basis for his receiving the award.

He proceeded to entertain us with stories about some of his in-country escapades. Apparently, he impressed his Captain with his willingness to take on any assignment, no matter how far outside of Air Force regulations they might've fallen. Jim stated that was the basis for the award.

After serving in Vietnam, Jim returned to CONUS (military jargon for Continental United States) and was assigned to McClellan Air Force Base in Sacramento. In that duty station, from August 1967 until September 1968, Jim went back to computers and was in charge of 35 keypunch operators.

After serving four years in the Air Force, Jim obtained his separation papers in September 1968 and began his higher education at Harbor Junior College in Wilmington, California. He graduated from that college with honors.

Jim then attended Long Beach State, where he graduated in 1972 with a BA degree in Economics.

Upon his graduation, Jim applied to the college's MBA program and started in 1973. However, he became disenchanted and dropped out.

Jim's next intended educational stop was applying to law school at South Western Law School, where he was accepted.

However, Jim, who was married at the time and working for Magnavox Research Labs, was experiencing marital problems and decided that law school would have to wait.

Being a great believer in Satchel Paige's life lesson to the effect that you have to keep moving or bad stuff is apt to catch up with you, while he was still working with Magnavox, Jim first obtained his real estate salesmen's license and then a real estate broker's license.

Jim continued working for Magnavox until 1978 when he accepted a position with Hughes Aircraft Company.

Jim started with Hughes as a Subcontracts Administrator, and then became the Head, International Subcontracts for the company.

While working in that capacity, the Hughes Group's legal counsel was impressed by Jim's work and suggested that he go to law school. To augment the proposal, she told Jim that she thought she could get Hughes to pay for Jim's law school.

This gal had gone to the University of West LA for her law degree. Since it was in Culver City, close to El Segundo where he was working, Jim applied and was accepted.

And the lady delivered. Hughes did pay for Jim's entire legal education.

Of course Jim, being Jim, didn't get his law degree and then take the bar exam like everyone else. He did it in the reverse order.

He took and passed the bar exam on his first try.*[The California Bar Association prides itself in offering the toughest bar exam in the country – often lawyer wannabes have to take the exam multiple times before they finally get to hang up their shingle.]*

However, unlike everybody else I've ever known who became a lawyer, Jim achieved that status *before* he graduated from law school! He was sworn in as a full-fledged lawyer two days before he graduated! I have no idea how you can do that.

What Jim had done was finish his law school coursework in December 1984. He applied to take the February bar exam in 1985 and passed on the first try. His class' graduation exercise took place after the lawyer swearing-in ceremony.

The President of the law school was Justice Bernard Jefferson, a gentleman who is famous in legal circles, particularly among trial lawyers, for writing the definitive judges' reference book on trial evidence.

According to Jim, Judge Jefferson was surprised and bemused by Jim's successful passage of the first California bar exam that he took. He admitted to Jim that he was surprised, because Jim had not exactly been one of his outstanding students in the Judge's evidence class at the law school.

Jim's response was a classic "Jimism." Jim reminded the Judge that Jim operated under the philosophy of MCE, *minimum critical effort!*

After becoming an attorney, Jim returned to his work at Hughes Aircraft.

Upon his return, much to the disgust of his supervisor, he received a 15% pay raise because now he had a Doctorate (LLD).

He continued to work for Hughes for another 15 months.

Jim then left and hung up his shingle as a sole practitioner in Torrance.

Practicing by yourself when you're a new lawyer is beyond challenging. Fortunately, after about a year, he joined Kemper Insurance as a trial attorney, working for an old law school buddy.

Three years after he joined Kemper, he was given the opportunity to open the Kemper Insurance Litigation Office in San Diego. He was the managing attorney for Kemper at that office for 13 years, until the company stopped writing liability insurance in 2003.

At this juncture in Jim's preparation of his resume for me, he apparently ran out of steam.

He listed that after the Kemper employment, he went to work for the Bacalski, Bailey, Koska, and Ottoson firm. Without further ado, he then stated: "Private practice, then finally to Nationwide until I retired."

Then, just to titillate your author, he offered the following:

"Too many sailing, diving and fishing adventures to list here. I did obtain my Coast Guard 100-ton Masters License in 1998. Held the license through three issues until I decided not to renew in 2014."

Then, with the obvious intent of adding insult to injury with this abrupt ending, Jim stated:

"There is plenty more, however I'm tired of typing now and think I'll have a cocktail. If you want more, I can supply it."

On a more serious note (finally Charley!), I personally viewed the information that Jim had finally found a lot on which to build his retirement home down in Western Florida as very much a good news/bad news situation.

The good news is that after years of exhaustive investigation and earning countless air mileage rewards, Jimmy and his wife have finally found the perfect location for building their retirement dream home with a dock, affording Jim incredible fishing within easy striking distance.

All of the bad news is on our side. Our Tuesday Morning Gang will be losing a wonderful friend and extraordinary raconteur. We can only hope that maybe Jim and Yuma Bill will have occasional reunions on Tuesday mornings at the Cardiff Seaside Market with our gang.

- fourteen -
Charley Marvin

Last, and definitely least, a little history about the compiler of this compendium.

Born in New Haven, Connecticut, at the tail end of the Depression. Raised from the time that I was a toddler until college in a little Connecticut country town of 2,500 New England Yankees, called Woodbridge. I'm not sure about the population count because they may have mistakenly included some dairy cows in the census.

Oldest of four boys. Growing up it was all about sports in our family.

My dad ran track at Yale and was a fairly accomplished baseball and hockey player when he was in high school. He loved all sports and passed on that love to his sons.

Football in the fall, basketball, hockey, and swimming in the wintertime, and baseball in the spring and summer, along with more swimming in the summer. That's the way our family marked the seasons.

My dad, being the sports nut that he was, built a basketball court on our driveway. He also constructed a baseball diamond, with a pitcher's mound no less, in our backyard.

As demonstrated by the long fly ball I hit through my mother's bedroom window, nearly impaling her with shards of flying glass, my father's ball diamond lacked a sufficient dimension in right field.

When I was in the third grade, my dad and a friend of his organized some local kids into a baseball team. Back in the late 40s, we didn't have any Little Leagues organized in our area. Instead, we played games against other teams from the surrounding small towns.

Later our team was taken over by a very savvy, Harvard MBA, who had made so much money in his insurance business that he could devote most of his afternoons to coaching me and the other knuckleheads on our baseball team. He actually knew something about baseball, and our team beat just about every team in that region.

We went to school in the little Woodbridge town elementary school, and grew up in an absolute *Leave it to Beaver* bubble.

Then, for junior high school, we were suddenly parachuted into the midst of a ghetto school in downtown New Haven. Quite a shock to a country kid!

Although I had some close calls, I managed to survive that year and one more year at a local high school in New Haven, Hillhouse High.

Then, serendipity stepped boldly into my young life. One of my dad's childhood friends, who had gone overseas with his dad who was stationed all over the world with the State

Department, took over a local prep school, Hopkins, as the headmaster.

He asked my dad if he had any kids who would like to go to the school, if they were able to earn scholarships. Providentially, in response, my dad pointed at me.

It was fortunate because my attendance at that rather prestigious private school, which, having been founded in 1660 is the second oldest continuously-operating educational facility in the United States, other than Harvard, eventually got me admitted to Yale and Amherst College, and higher education points beyond.

While matriculating at Hopkins, I was able to continue my life-long love of sports.

I played football until I wiped out the medial meniscus in my right knee as a junior.

I was also a (very) short distance freestyle swimmer and the anchorman on the school's freestyle relay team. I thought my dad was going to bust a gut in his excitement when, at the Yale pool, I managed to win the New Haven County 50-yard free-style swimming event against the area's other top sprinters.

Of course he also thought I won the 100-yard freestyle championship in the same meet.

However, due to the fact that I tanked after about half of the race, at the end of the contest I faded terribly and nearly drowned before another swimmer and I had what were apparently nearly simultaneous touches at the finish.

Swimming endurance wasn't my forte.

I continued playing baseball at the prep school. I had some success as a pitcher. As a matter of fact, in my senior year, I somehow managed to pitch a perfect game against our archrivals, Choate.

Eleven strikeouts and no walks.

[As an aside, and apropos of absolutely nothing, unfortunately that is one and the same prestigious Connecticut private school, Choate, that you've been hearing about lately on national TV. Choate's national notoriety is a function of all of the school's historical sexual shenanigans involving some members of their faculty with their students.]

Talk about excited. My dad was still bragging about that no-hitter, not years, but rather decades, later. That's when he presented me with the baseball that I had used in pitching that perfect game. After all those many years, I had no idea that he had what he (and only he!) considered a treasured sports artifact.

———

I don't want you to think that the no-hitter went to my head. I'm here to share with you that any bragging I may have contemplated was quashed three days later when I pitched against the Yale freshman baseball team.

To be mercifully brief, my infielders and I were lucky to get out of that game with all of our limbs still securely attached to the appropriate joints of our bodies. Those guys were hitting rockets all over the field!

You might consider three days a quick turnaround for a young pitcher. Actually it was. I had a real salami arm that day. However, acknowledging that there wasn't much depth in our team's pitching staff would have been a gross understatement.

———

This private school had extremely high academic standards and some really smart students. Since I didn't exactly fit that mold, I had my first exposure to absolutely never being the smartest guy in the room.

Unfortunately, this same intellectual handicap tracked my academic career all the way through Amherst College, and onto law school, at the University of California, Berkeley.

When the Dean of Admissions at Berkeley (Boalt Hall) talked to us the first day of our law school classes (as I recall he was interrupted by Mario Savio and his Free-Speech Gang busting through our lecture hall), he started off by telling us all how smart we were. He then made some inane statement about summa cum laude's and Phi Beta Kappa's being on either side of each of us first year law students.

Hearing that, I immediately looked at my neighbors on both sides and confessed to them that, at least in my particular instance, no ever-loving way the Dean was correct!

———————

I was shocked by my admission to Yale. Maybe the fact that my dad was a Yale alumnus, same for my headmaster, and the fact that our private school fed half of each of its graduating classes to Yale, had a little something to do with it. Ya think . . . ?

But I decided that I wanted to "go away to college." So instead of driving 7 miles from my home to attend Yale, I decided to accept a scholarship to attend Amherst. After all, it was definitely going away to school, because it was at least 90 miles from home, all the way up in Massachusetts.

Well . . . upon reflection, I guess it's not really like I was going across the country to UCLA!

Some years following my graduation, I learned that I was barely admitted to Amherst. As a matter of fact, my Headmaster at Hopkins later advised me that he had a bet with the Dean of Admissions about the likelihood of my eventually graduating from Amherst.

Fortunately, my Headmaster won the bet and, following my graduation, the Amherst Dean of Admissions hosted a very fancy dinner for him.

Not that it wasn't a close thing.

At the end of my freshman year, I was advised by that same Dean that I was on probation because of my less than stellar grades. That was okay, because some of my classmates got to enjoy an involuntary year leave of absence from the college for the same academic deficiency reasons.

At Amherst, as a freshman, my overindulgence in my love for sports may have impacted my less than stellar academic performance. I competed on the freshman swimming team, as well as pitching on the freshman baseball team.

With regard to swimming competitively, by the time I was a freshman in college, I had decided that I liked breathing while I was swimming. Therefore, I switched from a freestyle sprinter to a backstroker.

At the end of that season, something occurred in our final swim meet against our archrivals, Williams, which made my decision to drop swimming the following year relatively easy to make.

I came in second in the backstroke event. Normally that would be an acceptable, even a laudatory result.

However, one problem. The guy that beat me only had one leg!

Yep, no doubt about it. As a sophomore, time to focus solely on baseball and my pitching!

I did okay as a pitcher at the school. During one summer break, I played on a semi-pro team with some fantastic athletes. My centerfielder was an All-American football player from West Point. I struck out 17 batters in one game and had a summer record of seven wins and two losses.

Thought I was pretty hot stuff until, the following spring, when I met with the Amherst varsity baseball coach. After watching me for a few minutes, he had crushing news. He advised me in no uncertain terms that I was a two-bit thrower and I didn't know how to pitch!

He went on to give me the fabulous news that we were going to have to start all over again with my pitching mechanics. In other words, the pitching motion that I had been using with some measure of success since I was in third grade, was totally useless by the time I became a sophomore in college.

By my senior year, the coach thought that I might have a breakout year pitching.

For him to even consider me anything more than a thrower, was really cool. The reason was the coach was widely recognized as one of the Deans of American college baseball coaching. As a matter of fact, right after World War II, the Boston Red Sox tried to make him their manager.

This guy coached the baseball team at Amherst from about the time of World War I until the mid-1960s!

His response to the Red Sox was a polite "thanks but no thanks." He went on to explain that he didn't want to leave the college game. He enjoyed working with college kids too much.

When I was a senior, one day at baseball practice in the Cage, just before our baseball team took its Spring Break swing south to play other college baseball teams in Florida, for all intents and purposes my competitive baseball career ended.

Ever since I had the operation to remove the medial meniscus from the football injury when I was a junior in high school, I had always had problems with my right knee.

Every few months I would twist the bloody thing, and it would balloon up so it looked like I had a basketball for a knee. The treatment was rather barbaric. A huge horse needle syringe pulling all that blood and gore out of the knee area.

Physically, other than my knee, up to that point I had stayed in good health throughout my athletic career.

During that particular practice, I was fielding grounders and making throws to first base. On one play, I threw awkwardly to the first baseman. A crunching sound in my elbow, lots of pain, and, worst of all, I immediately had a dead arm.

Knowing a little more about pitchers' elbows today, it's pretty clear to me that at that moment in time I was an excellent candidate for Tommy John surgery. Unfortunately, however, because at that time Tommy was probably still in elementary school, his pitching arm saving surgery was still unknown to orthopedic surgeons!

———————

Sadly, not wanting to miss Spring Break in Florida, I have to acknowledge that I was less than forthright with our baseball coach about my right elbow injury.

Back in those days, no matter how you were injured, or where you were injured, most athletes figured that you would heal if you ran enough miles.

I'm here to report that I ran my ass off down in Florida!

But, for some crazy reason, all of that running didn't have any beneficial effect on my right elbow!

The moment of truth came when the coach named me as the starter in a spring game, up against the formidable Ohio State varsity baseball team.

When the coach advised me of that fantastic opportunity, I accurately anticipated a veritable train wreck about to occur on the baseball diamond.

———————

Like the game I pitched against the Yale freshman baseball team, I made the Ohio State batters look like they were all ready to play in the Major Leagues. Their hitters' cannon shots were caroming all over that baseball field and over the fences.

By the second inning, my first and third basemen were begging for mercy!

———————

The baseball lesson that I learned that day is this. As a pitcher, when you have about 50% of your normal fastball velocity, and your damaged elbow won't let you throw a curve, and you're pitching against really good hitters, the players on the other team should be required to have to make some rather large side payments to you.

The reason is the fabulous false impressions that all of the Major League scouts in the stands were receiving about the Ohio State players' hitting prowess!

_____

Sadly, after we got back to school in Massachusetts, I had to inform the baseball coach that my arm was shot, thus ending my organized baseball career.

One of the saddest days of my life.

Looking back now, I'm pretty sure I know the genesis of my career-ending elbow injury. I had been throwing curveballs, and every other pitch that I could imagine, starting when I was only in the third grade.

Because most of the teams that I played on didn't have more than one or two pitchers, the number of pitches I threw through grammar school, high school, American Legion, not to mention college and summer semi-pro- ball, would give today's youth baseball managers a severe case of apoplexy!

_____

When I was about 60 and I needed to have my right shoulder replaced, my orthopedic surgeon couldn't figure out why my shoulder was so badly damaged.

He knew I was heavily into road biking and asked me if I'd

had a biking accident. I advised him in the negative. *[I had a beauty some years later, doing an Endo on Bob Hope Drive in the desert. Ambulance trip to Eisenhower Hospital with a concussion (for a while I couldn't remember where we were staying or how Kirsten could be contacted), broken collarbone, full body road rash, and a basketball size swelling on my left hip that lasted for many months. However, that little train wreck occurred well after I had my right shoulder replaced.]*

Nope, I told him, I didn't have a bike wreck. But I did go on to explain to him that I started pitching and throwing curveballs when I was in the third grade, and pitched all the way through college.

The doctor's immediate response was a simple and resigned: "Oh, that explains it!"

When I graduated from Amherst I didn't have a clue about what I was going to do next. Something like 87% of my graduating class members were destined to go on to graduate school. Given my limited intellectual capacity, it took no time for me to determine that graduate school was not my best option.

So of course I joined the Navy!

Went to Pensacola, Florida, right after graduation, to go through OCS (Officer's Candidate School) with all the fly boys . . . the pilots and navigators. My class was the first one that had Air Intelligence Officers mixed in with the Junior Birdmen.

My primary purpose in joining the Navy was to avoid further over taxation of my circumscribed intellect. Of course, in its infinite wisdom, the Navy decided that during my 4-½ years as an active duty naval officer, I should spend the first 18 months going through OCS and advanced intelligence schools. That's about the equivalent of over two of the three years of graduate law school!

Not only that, but I spent the last 14 months of my naval career as an instructor in an Air Intelligence Training Center at NAS Alameda, in the Bay Area.

Therefore, my education evasion plans missed the mark by a tad. Out of the some 54 months of my active duty in the Navy, about 32 months of that time was spent either going to school or teaching in a Navy school.

The best laid plans . . .

———————

But heck, I can't complain. During the year and a half that I was actually acting like a real naval officer, the Navy stuck me on the island of Guam, in the middle of the godforsaken Pacific Ocean!

———————

Now I could regale you with some rather ribald tales about the airline stewardesses that I met when their planes arrived in Guam; crazy experiences while on leave in the Philippines and Japan; and the like. However, once again we have to keep in mind that this narrative is rated PG.

———————

As I was contemplating leaving the Navy, running out of any other viable options (I certainly didn't want to go out and get a real job!), I took the LSATs and applied to UC Berkeley Law School. As I noted earlier, I managed to get admitted by the skin of my teeth!

I paid my way through law school by being on the G.I. bill, becoming a member of the US Navy Reserve, working at the school's law library, and was a mid-20-year-old hasher to a bunch of girls in a sorority who thought they were God's gift to the universe. A long step down from my previous experience being a naval officer, waited on hand and foot, 24/7, by Philippino stewards!

Between my second and last year of law school, shortly after I became a full Lieutenant in the Navy Reserves, I resigned my Navy commission.

I made that decision because this was the time when the Vietnam War was really heating up. The Navy was calling up Air Iintelligence Officer Reserves (my Navy MOS) to serve on Navy carriers in the Gulf of Tonkin, off of the coast of Vietnam.

MY MESSAGE TO THE US NAVY: *NOT BEFORE THE LAST YEAR OF LAW SCHOOL, YOU DON'T!!!*

After barely getting into law school, I then I managed to top that off with a totally undistinguished law school career!

Because of my exposure to San Diego while I was in the Navy, my first choice after I got my law degree was to get a job in that wonderful city. However, my C grades in law school did not elicit a great deal of enthusiastic interest on the part of San Diego law firms.

Fortunately I was able to land a law associate job with a large downtown Los Angeles law firm.

The only good thing about that job was that we got to live in Marina del Rey, which was then, in the latter part of the 1960s, party central. Then we moved to that other party central Mecca, Manhattan Beach.

[Okay gang, please take note of the fact that I did have the requisite South Bay connection!]

While working with the LA firm, I did everything from grunt work in workmen's compensation cases, defending Pacific Tel & Tel and Standard Oil, to bag carrying on some huge national antitrust class-action cases, working for the senior guy in the firm, who was one of the leading antitrust lawyers in the country. Working for him, I assisted in defending General Motors and Bristol-Myers, among others.

In Manhattan Beach, we bought a duplex at 613 Manhattan Beach Boulevard, just up from the pier. That gave me a chance to launch my lifelong love of the ocean, beach volleyball, and body surfing.

After some four years with the LA firm, when I was informed that I was going to be making partner within the next year, I did the only prudent thing I could think of.

I immediately took a 10-day vacation in San Diego, seeking legal employment in our fair city.

During that compacted ten-day period, I must've pounded on almost 20 small law firm doors, seeking employment. Because of my LA legal experience with a large firm, I had decided that I wanted to work with a small law firm instead.

Nobody was hiring in San Diego in early 1971. I tried to get hired by small firms, but drew a blank every time. I guess I should've been excited, because nearly every time a door was slammed in my face, it was just after the attorney had told me that I had some fairly impressive legal credentials.

On the last day, I interviewed with a firm that I would've loved to be hired by. Long story short, they said they would hire me in one year. My quick response was that I couldn't wait a year because I would be a partner in the LA law firm by then.

Fortunately, on that last day of our vacation, I was talking with Larry Irving. Larry was a partner in that firm who went on to become a highly-respected US Federal District Court Judge, and, after he did the unheard-of by quitting his lifetime federal judicial assignment (he had a disagreement with the federal mandatory sentencing requirements), became an obscenely well-paid national arbitrator of huge cases.

Larry informed me that he could get me a job that day if I was willing to change my targeting and accept employment by a large firm. As a matter of fact, he promised me that I would have a job within half an hour after he made a phone call.

Since I either elected to grab this life-saving flotation ring or I was probably doomed to spend the balance of my career toiling in downtown LA, thank God I acquiesced.

True to his word, 30 minutes after Larry had made the phone call, I had been hired as a new associate at Higgs, Fletcher, and Mack!

And the rest as they say is history . . .

Sorry about that, but I'm not done yet. For those of you who will be complaining about the fact that I wrote more about myself that I did about other members of our esteemed group, I have this admonishment.

I'm more familiar with the subject of this narrative than I was with any of the protagonists of the other biographies that I worked on!

Not only that, but you guys were really skimpy on giving me a lot of details about your lives! As a matter of fact, if the truth be known, because of the lack of background information, I was forced to make up most of your life narratives!

Again, trying mightily, but with very limited success, to limit the length of this biography, I will just quickly list below a sampler of the stories that I *will not be writing about in this narrative.*

- One summer, between college semesters, a friend of mine and I drove across the USA and Canada, working in a Kansas wheat elevator and on the Colorado Highway Patrol;

- One night on the same trip, smashing into and killing a 10-point buck, while traveling at 75 miles an hour with the convertible top down, on the Trans-Canada Highway, outside of Moose Jaw, Saskatchewan;

- At 3:00 a.m. that same night in Moose Jaw, the two of us escaping from the amorous tentacles of a gay cowboy who was 6'8" tall and weighed about 260 pounds of muscle;

- The hurricane that hit New England when I was a teenager, with so much rainfall that we had railroad boxcars floating down local rivers and demolishing cement bridge overpasses;

- The night that Typhoon Karen hit Guam, when I was the Squadron Duty Officer, with winds over 200 miles an hour;

- The tornado that struck our Neptune Avenue beach home in November 1972, tore off our roof and deposited it around the neighborhood, as well as out in the street, causing such extensive damage that it was almost 5 months before our home was repaired sufficiently to move back in;

- Seven consecutive years of Tecate to Ensenada bicycle races, most of which, because of the excessive ingestion of alcohol, I can't remember;

- Some pretty radical body surfing wave riding, including one morning having my spine shortened in an impenetrable fog bank, when my heels were slammed into the bluff after riding on an absolutely monstrous wave, which I never was actually able to see;

Well I think you get the drift . . .

To finish up on my legal career, I spent six years with Higgs, Fletcher, and Mack, until 1979, and became a partner in the firm in 1974.

I started in the downtown office and then pioneered the first North County office opened by a large San Diego law firm. I opened that office in 1973 in Escondido and managed that satellite facility through 1979, building the office to eight attorneys.

Initially I was doing trial work for the firm, but, being so bloody smart that I could see the real estate boom coming for the North County (having lived in the LA beach areas for five years, that was a real leap of faith . . . Yeah DUHH!), I transitioned out of trial work into becoming a transactional lawyer doing business and real estate law work.

Even though I was living on Neptune in Leucadia at the time, I spent so much time in Escondido that they thought I was a native. They even made me President of their Chamber of Commerce in 1978.

In 1979, I left the Higgs firm and formed my own firm, Marvin, Huiskamp & Black, with two of my Higgs partners, over in Rancho Santa Fe, above the old Quimby's restaurant. My partner, Charles Black, eventually ended up as the attorney and advisor for John Moores, helping him ramrod the entire Petco Park, and environs, project.

In 1984, when our lease ran out, we split up and I

brought an associate with me and opened another law firm in Encinitas.

That wasn't the only split I made that year. After 18 very tumultuous years of marriage, I began divorce proceedings from my first wife. As luck would have it, I met Kirsten on a blind date about four months later, and once again, as they say, the rest is history . . . I finally got it right!!

I met and married my life soulmate!

Fortunately, starting back in the early 1970s, I acquired a fascination for real estate investments along Coast Highway 101. Everyone else thought I was crazy. My friends were all buying second homes as investments.

At one time, by the early 1980s, my ex and I owned about 2/10s of a mile of frontage along 101 in Leucadia and downtown Encinitas. The properties included: the first commercial property on the North end of the Coast Highway in Leucadia that presently includes the Mexican restaurant; the property just north of gas station; the Papagayo restaurant property; the 12-unit apartment house up above Papagayo, towards Beacons Beach; the Gold Coast Plaza property on the South side of the the Pannikin; and the property that Don Hansen keeps bitching at me about at our meetings, the classic car property to the immediate North of his store.

Over the years, I've owned four different motels, although now, with the last unit, the Leucadia Beach Inn, we're real hoity-toity because we added the word "Inn" instead of "Motel."

Just to prove my bona fides as a real estate investment guru, in the late 1970s I made a brain-dead investment in a 28-unit motel in Desert Hot Springs. I made that incredible selection instead of buying another motel that I was looking at, *on the South end of El Paseo, in Palm Desert!!*

My rationale for that purchase was faultless. I wanted an excuse to take my family to the desert on the weekends.

Good thinking Charley!!

Not only that, but I bought the damn place from a Bible-thumping group of Romanians who had escaped across the Iron Curtain.

They proceeded to convince this self-proclaimed really smart lawyer that since "in the old country we don't keep books because the government steals from us," they didn't have any books for me to review. Great call Charles!

However, Jim Thompson and Bill Taggart, who have had substantial legal experience of their own during their careers, I want you guys to rest easy. I'm here to tell you that I never ever would've committed legal malpractice by actually advising a client to do that!

Through the property investments, I was cruising for retirement by the time I was 50, until I got a divorce when I was 46. PFFTTT!!! went a lot of real nice property. In addition, she got to keep our beach house on the North end of Neptune. It is situated only 2, much-too-short miles, North of the home that I bought as we were separating, at 200 Neptune, on the South end of the street.

That's where Kirsten and I have lived for the last 32 years.

Then, once again, to amply demonstrate that the legal doctor needed to "heal thyself," I joined two other guys to form a real estate development company, just in time to catch the Savings and Loan national tsunami in the late 1980s!

Not only was my timing terrible, but my choice of partners was even worse! Those two SOBs really took this crackerjack, self-styled, ace attorney, to the cleaners!

We did joint venture the development of the mixed-use project just east of the Solana Beach train station. That was a nice project. We also built the office building where I had my law practice for 15 years, in back of the Jack-in-the-Box, at 120 Birmingham, in Cardiff.

I'm really proud about the way I handled the third project that we started, in Lemon Grove.

Fortunately (not for the client but for me as an object lesson!), I had a former client in Long Beach who dropped something north of $1 million because of a UPS oil dump, which occurred while that company was leasing his property.

Armed with that irrefutable proof of the financial dangers inherent in the presence of hazardous materials, I bailed from the Lemon Grove project during escrow when our due diligence disclosed a gasoline plume under the property that had migrated from a neighboring gas station. I was more than happy to let my two nefarious partners keep my initial deposit of a few thousand dollars, as money well spent.

After I bailed on that project, I learned that traffic was stopping on Highway 94 because of the Grand Canyon being dug adjacent to the freeway by my ex-partners. I think they finally had to remove and dispose of about 10,000 cubic yards of contaminated material.

At least I dodged one real estate investment bullet!

———————

So let's review my extremely convoluted march towards a planned retirement.

Instead of retiring at age 50, I got a divorce. I figured at the time, oh what the heck, now I'll have to wait till age 55.

Then I figured out how to screw that up too. I became a real estate developer at the absolutely wrong time. Now I was looking at my 60s to escape from the all-consuming tentacles of my law practice.

Ultimately, in reality, only two very lucky real estate investments permitted me to retire at age 67!

So much for personally directed long-term retirement planning!

———————

Although I've made some world-class, Hall of Fame, dumb decisions in my life, at least I not only found the love of my life in Kirsten, but also one extremely talented designer.

Kirsten, in her capacity as an extraordinary designer, is not afraid of large pallets. She has transformed a former motel property into a chic retail center.

Not only that, but she took a dated motel (a portion of the Inn was built in the 1920s and is the oldest continuously operated lodging facility in the city of Encinitas), and through her marvelous redesign and remodeling skills, created a very popular destination niche Inn.

And she wasn't done yet. She then took on a really big project and worked on the redesign and remodeling of our medical building, located directly across from the YMCA ballfields, on Saxony, in Encinitas.

And, oh yeah, she did some pretty spectacular remodeling of our nearly 50-year-old home on the beach.

————————

Along the way, Kirsten and I have owned three different stores. One, during the 1980s, was a high-end ladies clothing store in the Lumberyard.

We had a reverse buyout from that investment! By that I mean we had to pay back credit card customers who'd been ripped off by Kirsten's partner.

————————

Our last store was the best. Kirsten opened the Epicurean, which was generally acknowledged by the locals as the best store in Idllywild. Fancy ladies' clothing, antiques, gifts, a cool wine cellar, and upscale cheeses, to enjoy on our elevated deck deep in the forest, looking down on the Strawberry Creek, to the accompaniment of Spanish flamingo guitarists!

————————

When I retired in 2005 and became a member of this esteemed group of characters, I looked back on my legal career and realized I had been blessed. Fortunately, in the late 1980s, when I advised my dad that I was becoming a developer, he immediately responded by offering the following sage advice:

> "Don't forget who brought you to the dance; your legal career!"

Over my career, I was fortunate to have a number of very cool clients.

They included Mr. Calloway of golf and wine fame; a lady who owned 1700 acres in Vista that became the Shadow Ridge housing development, along with quite a bit of industrial development property; Mitsui Fudasan, the developer of over 500 acres of industrial buildings, East of the Carlsbad Raceway; and Ted Gildred, the developer of Lomas Santa Fe, as well as the majority of the commercial properties in Solana Beach. I represented his company in acquiring the 600-acre industrial parcel between the Carlsbad Airport and the Carlsbad Raceway, and a 17-acre parcel across from UTC that I helped his company acquire, develop, and lease. I did the Marshall's lease for Ted, etc. etc.

Not to mention, among my clients, the world's coolest NFL GM, Bobby Beathard!!

Through a real quirk, I ended up as the real estate attorney for Relational Investors. For that company, I negotiated a lease for two full floors, totaling more than an acre of office space, on top of a high-rise office building in Carmel Valley.

Ralph Whitworth, the owner of the company, and the gentleman who I worked with on those projects, went on to become the Chairman of the Board of Waste Management and then Chairman of the Board of Hewlett-Packard. Sadly, he died recently of brain cancer.

This quiet accountant type, was an interesting character. Ralph was particularly accomplished when it came to birthday gifts for his wives.

For his first wife's 50th birthday, he closed down the village of Rancho Santa Fe for a private performance by Paul McCartney and his band. That cost him a cool million dollars contribution to McCartney's favorite charity.

Then, so that his second wife wouldn't get her knickers in a knot, for her birthday party he had a private performance at the Belly Up Tavern . . . by none other than Mick Jagger and the Rolling Stones!!!

And you know what's really weird about all this? I was never that accomplished of an attorney. I was okay, but I was still that middle of the pack, Gentleman C, graduate from Berkeley.

Basically I was just a country lawyer, a sole practitioner for the last 15 years, from the little town of Encinitas.

I certainly had my share of fence line disputes between neighbors, minor land-use planning issues with various government agencies, and other small town legal minutia which are part of the everyday fair for all country lawyers.

Just lucky I guess . . .

With our bunch of (older) surfers, each of our biographies has to have at least one surf story. That's the rule and I don't want to be criticized for being the first one to violate it.

Here's my surf story, and it's not about me. It's about my oldest daughter, Natasha.

In 1985, right in the throes of my divorce, Kirsten and I decided to send Natasha on a student exchange program to Salvador, Bahia, in Brazil. We thought it would be a good idea to get Natasha out of the free fire zone of the divorce proceedings.

Natasha was 16 years old at the time and went to Brazil for her Junior year in high school. She was accompanied by her life-long friend, Christie.

Salvador, Bahia, is known for being one of the top surfing spots in all of Brazil. The city itself has about 50 miles of pristine beaches.

Natasha and her younger sister, Tara, literally grew up on the beach, on the North end of Neptune.

Our home had a stairway down to the beach, and the kids and I spent most of our free time down on the sand or out in the water. In the summertime, all of the kids' friends would join them down on the beach and out surfing.

From the time when they were toddlers, I had my girls out in the water all the time. I started them off on boogie boards and then quickly they graduated to surfboards.

I couldn't surf with them because I've always had balance problems. The physical problem eventually manifested itself into my present condition of peripheral neuropathy. However, I was a fairly accomplished body surfer, and most mornings, before work, was out in the water year-round without a wetsuit.

I absolutely loved the ocean, and still do!

In any event, I was able to get those kids up on waves when they were still little gremmies.

Both of them became quite accomplished surfers. Natasha won most of the local surf contests she entered. But her younger sister, Tara, as she grew older, began giving Natasha, who is two years older, a real run for her money.

———

While Natasha was getting ready to leave for Brazil, she asked me if she should bring her surfboard. Without giving the matter a lot of thought, I came up with an absolutely inane response. As I was looking at this cute little 16-year-old girl, I stated: "If you want to meet some boys, of course you'll want to take your surfboard to Brazil!"

Terminally dumb remark by a supposedly responsible father!

———

Once Natasha reached Brazil, it wasn't long before, at her insistence, the extended brothers and cousins of the two families that she was staying with, invited her and Christie to go surfing with the gang.

At the time, they initially assumed the two girls were some lightweight, wannabe, surfer girls from Southern California.

It didn't take more than one outing with Natasha and Christie for the boys to quickly recognize that they could outsurf most of them.

———

Having observed their level of surfing talent, they suggested that the two girls enter a woman's surf contest that was scheduled to be held in the city.

The girls agreed to give it a go.

It was a full-on surf tournament covering four days. The two girls kept winning their heats and by the end of surfing on Saturday afternoon, had qualified for the semi-finals on Sunday morning.

Natasha won her semi-final heat but Christie didn't move on. After she won her semi-final heat, Natasha went out to water's edge to stretch prior to the beginning of the final.

Natasha reported that by that point on Sunday, the beach was absolutely mobbed. She stated that she hardly had room to do her stretching exercises in the shallow waters before the final. The reason was that there was such a mob of people packed in around her, taking photographs.

Things went well for Natasha during the final. She won the surf contest.

Then, according to Natasha, to her amazement all Hell broke loose.

Suddenly she was standing up at the edge of the beach with all manner of huge TV cameras and microphones thrust in her face, attempting to respond to questions being posed to her in Portuguese.

Now mind you, that posed a bit of a problem for her. The reason was that she had only been in the country for about three months. She didn't speak a word of Portuguese when she first arrived. Her Spanish wasn't too bad, but the Portuguese language is entirely different.

Somehow she survived the TV interviews and finally was proudly escorted back to their home by her very excited host family.

According to Natasha, when she reached the family's home, her family members were absolutely beside themselves with excitement. They couldn't stop talking about the wonderful thing that she had accomplished by winning the surf contest.

They then proceeded to tell her that her surfing and her interviews in broken Portuguese, that evening were going to be on local sports TV.

Natasha was shocked when she was told by the family that the same evening she would be on national sports TV out of Rio de Janeiro (think Brazilian national ESPN!). And she was!

By this point, Natasha related to me that her head was just spinning from all of this incredible information.

However, the family then managed to put the entire adventure over-the-top.

They asked her if she knew who the lady was that she had beaten in the final. Of course, Natasha answered in the negative, because she didn't have a clue.

That's when the family dropped the bomb on her.

"Natasha, in the final you just beat the Brazilian Woman's Surfing Champion!!"

A major Brazilian surfing contest won by a little 16-year-old girl from Leucadia. A little girl who later acknowledged to her dad that she would never have even been able to stand up on her surfboard, much less win the contest, if she had known who she was surfing against!

- fifteen -

Richard "Clarkie" Clark
[Emeritus Member]

Clarkie is another of our group's illustrious Emeritus Members. Sadly, it's about eight years since Clarkie last graced one of our meetings, shortly before he passed away in 2009.

I was in the Tuesday Morning Gang with Clarkie for about four years, until we lost him. Unfortunately, although he was always open and friendly, I never got to know too much about his background.

However, I did have a chance to get to know him well enough to appreciate what a terrific and caring guy Clarkie was.

Fortuitously, as is often the case with our group, we have a fellow member who goes *way back* with Clarkie.

That would be our beloved Woody.

Recently I spent an afternoon with Woody at his wonderful beachfront home in Leucadia. For those of you that haven't visited at Woody's home, if you get a chance, definitely accept the invitation. Woody's home is a surfing museum of photographs and memorabilia. During our conversations, every few minutes

Woody would stop me and run off and bring back a photograph that included the old-time surfers we were talking about.

When we got together at his home, first we talked about Woody's biography. Then Woody offered some insight into the life of his good friend, Clarkie.

———————

Clarkie was brought up on the beach in South Mission Beach. He was a Waterman from his early days.

Clarkie grew up to be a very prudent and successful real estate investor. According to Woody, he owned about a block of property on Mission Bay. He also owned commercial properties in downtown San Diego.

But his best real estate investment ever was initially buying two houses across from the Windansea surf break, in La Jolla. Eventually he bought a third house so that he owned all three of the homes that fronted on that block, adjacent to the intersection of Neptune and Bonaire.

More on Clarkie's spectacular beach house later.

———————

Clarkie graduated from Point Loma high school and competed as a swimmer at Occidental College.

Clarkie and Woody first got to know each other in the 1940s, surfing together at Windansea.

According to Woody, Clarkie was a fitness fanatic all through his life. He carefully watched his diet and was constantly working out through his paddling and surfing.

That explains why the dude looked so terrific, all the way into his 80s!

Woody indicated that Clarkie often worked out and practiced for long hours on his paddleboard on Mission Bay.

On one occasion, Woody, who was watching the incredible amount of exertion that Clarkie put into his paddling, asked him how he could continue his grueling regime.

Clarkie had a quick response: "You have to thrust against pain!" That mantra was adopted by the two of them during their later years of surfing adventures together.

Clarkie competed in the mainland to Catalina paddling contest, which, multiple years, Roy Bream, one of our more itinerant TMG members, won. I read about Roy winning the races in one of the old surfing journals

Any of the rest of you compete in that Catalina paddling contest? How did you do?

Clarkie's working career was primarily spent building up a business started by his dad. His dad's business was Wilson F. Clark Wholesale Hardware Co., located in San Diego.

Back in 1950, the hardware company had a key department. This department sold a small line of key blanks, padlocks and a few Ilco key machines. Back in those days, the company's market was very local and a few orders for the key department per day was a cause for serious celebration.

In 1953 that key department was transformed. A new corporation was formed under the name of CLARK Security Products. This new company was owned and operated by our Clarkie, who was right in the middle of that new business launch.

Clarkie developed the company into a reliable locksmith supplier, stocking a wide variety of commercial and residential security products.

He was so good at what he did, and had so much experience in that field, that, according to Woody, Clarkie wrote the "Locksmiths' Bible." In that handbook, he set forth detailed instructions for the installation, care, repair, and maintenance of various security locks.

Woody claims that even today, Clarkie's handbook is still in circulation among locksmiths.

Not only that, but according to Woody, Clarkie was one of the first local businessmen to pioneer using computers for inventory control.

Clarkie's company outlived him.

After over 30 years in the business, in 1983, he sold the business to a group of his company managers.

To quote from the company's website, this group of managers combined to enhance and expand the Clark tradition for caring about and assisting the locksmithing trade.

Their method was to set up a series of innovative programs designed to help locksmith owners grow their own businesses. The company is still carrying on that tradition today. I believe that it was a form of franchising, but I'm not certain about that.

In 2010 CLARK Security Products was purchased by Anixter international. This company is a *leading global distributor* of communication and security products.

Today, locksmiths affiliated with CLARK Security Products, have over 25,000 security devices available for their customers.

That sure is one hell of a long way from the company's genesis of getting excited about selling a few security products per day in Clarkie's Dad's hardware store key department back in the early 1950s!

Way to go Clarkie!!

I can offer a quick testimonial to the quality of the products produced by Clarkie's company.

In the early 1970s, when Woody built his own home on the beach on Neptune Avenue, he purchased all of the security hardware, which was installed in his home, from his old surfing buddy, Clarkie.

When I recently visited with him, Woody proudly pointed out some examples of those security products that are still in his home. I was amazed. They still all looked brand-new and obviously worked as well as they had when they came out of the box some 45 years ago.

As someone who also has a beach house, I'm here to tell you that every piece of security hardware in our home has rusted or otherwise failed. And our home was built at almost the same time as Woody's!

As best I can tell, the amazing condition of Woody's hardware was undoubtedly a combination of Woody's continued maintenance and Clarkie's superior products!

Woody and Clarkie first got to know each other in the late 1940s, surfing at Windansea.

They also had some experience together playing for the

Bohman Brothers Marching Band (the band's sponsor was a mortuary!) in San Diego. Woody played clarinet in the Junior Division, while Clarkie played drums in the Senior Division.

In addition to the surfing, they pulled off stunts like traveling downtown into San Diego early on Sunday mornings. They then would take an elevator up to the seventh and top floor of a parking garage and wildly ride their skateboards on the spiraling driveway all the way down to the ground floor. Then they would hop into the elevator again and head back up to repeat the process.

———

In the Prologue, I felt constrained to offer the reader a little background on the makeup of our group because I've come across another literary conundrum, one with which I wrestled for a great deal of time.

My problem is this. I look at the various guys who make up our Windansea contingent, and all I see are a bunch of consummate gentleman.

My conundrum is: How the heck does our guys' exemplary deportment square with the world infamous reputation, so well earned by other Windansea surfing legends, such as Butch Van Artsdalen, as world class, over-the-top, beyond the pale, bigger than life, screw ups!?

———

Most of us have seen the classic late 1950s Windansea group photo where each one of the subjects is demonstrating his personal IQ for the camera.

By the mid-50s, Windansea surfers had more than earned a

reputation for not only being fearless and talented in the water, but also rude and funny on the beach, as well as openly hostile to any visiting tourists.

An example of the latter. The following graffiti appeared on a wall at that iconic surfing site:

"Warning!!! Windansea may be hazardous to tourists!!"

How the heck do you go from that kind of inner-city playground mentality to the likes of Mike Burner, Woody and Carl Ekstrom, Tommy Carroll, and Clarkie, the complete gentlemen?

All from the same Windansea surfing mecca that bred the likes of Van Artsdalen and his merry band of nut cases!

This morning at our meeting I talked with Tommy Carroll about the dichotomy between the characters of our group's Windansea guys and Van Artsdalen, et all.

Tommy said there was a relatively simple answer. He said that, with the exception of Mike Burner, Tommy's group of Windansea alumni were older than Van Artsdalen and his bunch.

And besides, we all know that Mike Burner is definitely a cut above the crazies that were around during his era. At least we think that's true.

However, I do remember one morning at one of our meetings when I was talking to an old fireman friend of mine who worked under Mike at one time as a fireman. He suggested that Mike was hell on wheels until he attained the exalted position of Fire Chief!

In any event, Tommy Carroll stated that when he saw how wild and crazy the surfing was getting around Windansea, he began focusing his surfing on Makaha. Tommy was able to do that because he was flying to the islands as a pilot with Pan Am.

————————

Anyway, you've got to give this to the Windansea Surfing Nursery. It sure did produce some legends in the surfing industry.

Believe it or not, legend has it that at Windansea as a hot surfing spot, the waves weren't ridden until a *New York born surf pioneer*, Woody Brown, paddled out in 1937. You mean to tell me that the Windansea surfing saga all started with a guy from Nuu Yawk!!!?

He was followed by La Jolla natives Don Okey and Townsend Cromwell, one of Woody's BFFs, who paddled out to the break the very next day.

They were soon joined by our Woody, Dorian Paskowitz and John Elwell, among others.

The first iteration of the Windansea "Shack," was erected on the sandstone bluffs, in front of the break, in 1946. The shack eventually became iconic within the ever-evolving world of surfing.

Also from that surfing nursery came a number of long-board-era surfers who went on to make names for themselves all over the world.

They included the surfer and shaper Pat Curren, Mike Diffenderfer, as well as our very own surfer, designer, and shaper extraordinaire, Carl Ekstrom.

The iconic surfing spot also launched the meteoric career, and ultimate terminal wipeout, of switchfooter Butch Van Artsdalen.

Others learning their world-class surfing craft there included Mike Hinson, of *Endless Summer* stardom, and Buzzy Bent, who went on to become a co-founder of the Chart House restaurant chain.

The surfing culture magnetism of Windansea manifested itself most strongly in the 1960s. Although I have a little trouble getting my head around the following fact, believe it or not, Andy Warhol, the artist who made obscene amounts of money off a tomato can painting, filmed a surfing documentary there in 1967.

Furthermore, Tom Wolfe, one of America's premier writers of the 20th century, published his surfing version of the famous 1930s St. Louis Cardinals baseball team "Gas House Gang." That was the literary classic entitled the "Pump House Gang," describing the local Windansea surf carnival.

The rest of the history of this surfing mecca is epic.

And guess what!? Our very own Woody and Carl Ekstrom were there at the inception, and I assume towards the beginning, accompanied by Clarkie and Tommy Carroll. Furthermore, it wasn't long before Mike Burner was right in the middle of that legendary gathering of surfing characters.

However, I have to admit that I get a little exasperated with Mike sometimes. He is such a gentleman that he hasn't even ever shared with us any salacious Butch Van Artsdalen stories!

Clarkie's story would not be complete without a quick discussion concerning Clarkie's wonderful home, looking out over the Windansea surf break.

Ever since 2005, when I originally joined this merry band

of prevaricator's, I have heard all manner of stories about the Windansea surf break and Clarkie's spectacular home immediately across the street from the break.

However I'm embarrassed to acknowledge that prior to Clarkie's Memorial service, I had never actually visited the Windansea surf break. I have body surfed most of the beaches in the North County but, prior to hanging up my swim fins for the final time, I had never made it down to this iconic surf break.

Fortunately I didn't have any difficulty finding Clarkie's home, because I had Woody as my navigator.

As I imagine is the case with most people, when I first arrived at Clarkie's home and looked out over the point break, I was awestruck by the view.

Woody and I are blessed with pretty nice ocean views from our beachfront homes. However, short of having a home on 17 Mile Drive in Carmel, looking out over the lone Cypress, I would be hard-pressed to identify a more magnificent ocean view anywhere in California than Clarkie's. It was truly spectacular!

———

We're going to have to leave Clarkie now.

According to Woody, music played a big part in Clarkie's life. Wherever he is at this time, he's likely to be listening to his favorite music; records produced by the British big band conductor, Ted Heath. As Clarkie would put it: "How Sweet it is."

And always remember Clarkie's enduring wisdom about life. In his words, as quoted by Woody:

"Where you are is a function of the decisions you make."

- sixteen -

Jim "Kimo" Enright
[Emeritus Member]

In March, 2015, we lost Jim, extraordinary Waterman, athlete, raconteur, and scientist, at the age of 83 years young. However, Jim lives on in the hearts and memories of the members of the Tuesday Morning Gang.

Putting together an anthology of the biographies of the members of our group wouldn't be right without including Jim's story.

That story follows. *[Editor's note: Thanks to Mary Ann, the narrative appearing below has relied heavily on Jim's memorial materials. I have also had the benefit of considerable input from Jim's longtime buddy, Bob Burnside.]*

———

Where to start Jim's story? I'll go back to the beginning in a little bit, but first I have to share a personal experience that I had with Jim.

As noted above, Jim was an extraordinary athlete. Among his numerous athletic achievements, Jim was one hell of a bicyclist, even towards the end of his life when he was getting older.

[I use the term "older" to describe Jim. Since our gang is getting a bit long of tooth, I need to quickly dispel a rumor about the adverse impacts of our advancing years. My oldest granddaughter once shared with me a life lesson that only a six-year-old, in their infinite wisdom, can deliver. She stated: "Papa, you're getting older but you're not old yet. You're not old until you're a hundred years old!" Since none of our members are even approaching that longevity plateau, we are all still maintaining our age in the category of "older"!]

I ran into Jim out on the road while we were both still cycling. Jim must've been in his late 70s at the time. He asked me if I did much riding. I proudly informed him I'd been cycling up and down the coast from San Diego to San Clemente for some 35 years. I went on to brag about having competed in the Tecate to Ensenada bicycle race over seven consecutive years.

Hearing that, Jim suggested that we should do some cycling together since we only lived a block apart on Neptune. I enthusiastically agreed. At the time I felt comfortable that Jim was some years older than I was, and, furthermore, I thought I was a fairly accomplished cyclist.

Wrong again Charley!

I proceeded to ask him where he liked to go riding.

He then described his favorite morning bike ride. He started off heading east over the Encinitas foothills to the steepest La Costa hills, then headed south and topped off the mornings with a run-up the Torrey Pines grade a couple of times. Then a pleasant coastal ride up out of the lagoon in a northerly direction, back through Del Mar, and then back home.

Jim went on to explain his affinity for such tortured topography in his biking. He loved to climb steep hills!

I quickly thought about his morning biking routine and

immediately recognized the obvious. This older gentleman was clearly far above my road cycling pay grade!

In response to Jim's inquiry about my joining him on some of those little morning bike jaunts, I evasively changed the conversation to the joys of being a grandparent!

———

The next time I saw Jim on his bicycle, he looked like he had been trapped in a phone booth with an angry mama grizzly and her two cubs.

I think the gang will remember when the Enrights and the Beathards were in Amsterdam, Holland, and our unsuspecting Jim was bushwhacked by an escalator.

He had been absent from a couple of our meetings before I saw him out on his bicycle. He still looked like he was going to fall off of the bike at any moment, because he was so badly injured. He had massive scabs and scarring all over his body.

Of course that little assault on his body didn't keep him off his bike!

That's when I received a second reminder that our Jim was made of rather stern stuff.

———

Jim was born toward the beginning of the Depression, in March, 1932, to an Irish Catholic family, with a French mom. I'm certain that there was a heavy Irish familial influence. I feel comfortable in stating that because he had second cousins in County Limerick and County Kerry, Ireland. Not only that, but his Aunt Mary from Carlsbad, for whom he apparently devoted about a decade of his life assisting, bore the Shamrock encased name of Mary O'Kelly Gilmore. For me, the finishing Irish touch was that one of Jim's numerous nicknames was "Seamus."

Jim was born in Los Angeles. After he had graduated from Mount Caramel High School in 1949, his family moved to Portland, Oregon.

A year later, Jim returned to Southern California and completed his AA degree at El Camino College. During that timeframe, Jim took the challenging LA lifeguard swim exam in May of 1951.

After qualifying as a LA lifeguard, he worked for the County for five years, first at the Hermosa Beach 13th Street tower, then at the Hermosa Beach Lifeguard Headquarters.

It was around this time, when he was working with the county as a lifeguard in Hermosa Beach, that Jim first met his soon to be lifetime buddy and body surfing competitor, Bob Burnside.

Bob also worked for the Los Angeles County lifeguard service. However, he was working in the northern division, up in the Zuma Beach area.

A couple of stories about Jim and Bob's lifelong relationship later on in this narrative.

Jim performed well as a lifeguard and was offered full-time lifeguard employment by LA County in the fall of 1953. He didn't accept the offer because he was attending UCLA, majoring in astronomy and physics. However, he continued to work weekends and summers lifeguarding with LA County, until he received his bachelor's degree from UCLA in 1956.

Upon his graduation from UCLA, Jim was promptly scooped up by TRW as an advanced engineer working with computers.

He went back to graduate school at UCLA and earned his master's degree in astronomy in 1959.

———

Jim's working career was with a company called Aero Nu-Tronics (Aeronautics Division of Ford Motor Company), described by his family as a sophisticated engineering firm in Newport Beach.

He was initially recruited and hired as an astrophysicist, working in orbital mechanics and software engineering. He moved to Newport Beach and worked as an astrophysicist with the company (which was later acquired by Lockheed Martin), finally ending his career when he retired in 1986 as Division Projects Manager for the company.

[At this juncture I have to pose a somewhat embarrassing question for the rest of the members of the Tuesday Morning Gang. How did anyone so smart, armed with such a stellar advanced education, who had worked at such esoteric astrophysical projects, ever end up hanging around with a bunch of undereducated reprobates like us?]

———

Now we get to the really important part of Jim's life history: his never-ending love affair with the ocean.

Let's review that relationship throughout Jim's life.

Jim grew up in Manhattan Beach. Then, according to the family, the Hermosa Beach surf was breaking just outside of his back door from the age of 18. When he moved to Newport Beach, he found a home on the water. He then proceeded to raise a family in his beautiful Oceanside oceanfront beach house, which he built, located at 1439 South Pacific Street. Jim's final years were spent with Mary Ann in their gorgeous Neptune Avenue beach house, staring out over Stone Steps Beach, in Encinitas.

So let's summarize. With the exception of the one year

following his high school graduation that Jim moved with his family to Portland, Oregon, Jim spent his whole life living within a block of the ocean, if not with the Pacific lapping up to his doorstep.

———————

By the way, going through the biographical information provided by Jim's family, I found out why Jim was such an extraordinary bike rider. When he commuted to his job in Newport Beach from his Oceanside beach house, he would often ride his bike to and from that destination.

I'm not sure exactly what the one-way commuting distance is between those two locations. However I feel comfortable stating that the round-trip was certainly guaranteed to create one formidable bike rider, which in Jim's case is exactly what happened!

———————

Jim's family reports that Jim identified himself as a beach boy, growing up among a family of avid golfers.

Jim lived up to his self-description during his lifetime. After having a college education limited career as an LA County life guard, he had an opportunity to return to his first love, the Pacific Ocean, when he began living on the Strand in Oceanside in 1969.

Then, as reported by his family, he began a heavy involvement in community body and longboard surfing events. He was one of the original competitors in the World Body Surfing Championships held at the Oceanside Pier. Jim helped organize those competitions and managed to obtain sponsors to make the event sustainable.

And Jim wasn't just the organizer. According to the family, he won his age bracket on a boringly repetitive basis.

Quick thought. According to Bobby Beathard, he was usually the winner of his age group at the Oceanside World Bodysurfing Championship competitions. Since they're both about the same age, somebody's embellishing! Just Sayin . . .

OOPS! I just talked with Bob Burnside, Jim's buddy and longtime fellow bodysurfing competitor.

Because I just love to start a friendly discussion about past accomplishments on the part of our group members, I believe in my never-ending quest for complete transparency I am compelled to share the following with you.

———

Bob and Jim were about three or four years older than Bobby Beathard. Therefore, the two of them duked it out in their age group for a number of years, before Bobby advanced age wise into their age category.

Shortly thereafter, Bobby beat Bob Burnside. Apparently the defeat was so traumatic for Mr. Burnside that he retired as an active age group body surfing competitor! Just kidding! Well at least I think that's sort of the story.

Here comes the important part. Bob Burnside claims that he and Jim really became close buddies when they were fierce competitors in the early years of the Oceanside World Body Surfing Championships. In any event, according to the history provided by the family, Jim was able to reach the finals of the Championships year after year. He also won three World Body Surfing Championships and apparently dominated the Oceanside community's men's 45-54 age class in body surfing.

Jim continued to compete in local community body surfing contests for another 25 years and was often a judge at the Oceanside Championships.

————————

Here comes the complicated part. On the phone recently from his home up in Utah, Bob Burnside told me that he won 13 straight Oceanside World Body Surfing Championships. I'm sure that Bob will straighten me out on whether that was winning the overall body surfing championships or the championship for his age group.

Bob's version is that Jim only beat him once in the body surfing championships.

My conundrum as your stellar reporter and relentless fact checker is that, as noted earlier, Bob and Jim were in the same age group for a number of those years.

I'm sure I will be straightened out on this knotty matter before we finally go to press.

BTW, in fairness to Bobby and Jimmy, Bob Burnside was a full-time lifeguard for some 30 years. Spending all his time out in the ocean on the job might have given him a bit of a leg up when it came to the body surfing championships, don't you think?

Not only that, but according to a newspaper article that Bob sent me, it sounds like he was in incredible physical condition, well into his older years.

Not to say that Bobby and Jim weren't also incredible physical specimens in their own right!

————————

At this point in the story about Bob and Jim's fierce body surfing competition over the years, I need to introduce Wanda the Mermaid into this narrative.

According to Bob, Wanda periodically surfaced in their relationship, both during the body surfing competitions, and when they were skiing together.

———————

To avoid complete and total confusion on the part of our fellow Bored oops I mean *Board* Members, you probably need to first hear the back story about Wanda the Mermaid. Wanda the Mermaid was the creation of Bob Burnside's very fertile imagination.

According to Bob, here we have a 30-year lifeguard who was having a very difficult time convincing his own kids that it was safe to go out in the ocean beyond the breakers.

That conundrum led to Bob's creation of a fairy tale that he shared with his children.

The fairy tale went along the following lines.

One day Bob was paddling out to the Point Dune Buoy. It was a cold and foggy morning and through the mists Bob suddenly heard someone crying.

He looked around trying to discover the source of this sadness. It was then that he noticed that a woman was hanging onto the bell buoy. However, she wasn't an ordinary woman.

"She was a mermaid."

When he approached, the mermaid told him that she had been hit by a large ship and that her tail was badly cut. She was extremely worried that a shark would smell the blood and attack her. She looked mournfully at Bob and said: "Please help me get back to my cave."

Fortunately, Bob was able to place her on his paddleboard and, through the fog, the mermaid directed him back to her "Secret Magical Cave."

Bob reported to his daughters that the cave was jam packed with treasures and beautiful things. Bob proceeded to carefully place her on a Golden Bed, which Bob indicated was encrusted with pearls and shells.

He was then able to tend to her wounds.

Before Bob left the cave, the mermaid thanked him. She also told him that she would always be there for him and his children whenever they were in the ocean, ready to protect them against any dangers that they might encounter.

Bob's story for his daughters went on. He related to them that, in the years to come, whenever he was near the buoy, he would call out Wanda's name. As soon as he called out, she would surface and talk with him. Bob told his daughters that he and Wanda became very close friends. During that friendship, Wanda revealed to Bob all of the wonders of the sea that she lived in.

Bob concluded the fairy tale for his daughters by stating:

> "So remember, she will always be around you when you are in the ocean . . . Watching over you and your safety. Maybe if you call her name softly, she may surface and give you a kiss . . . BUT she will always be close to you."

In discussing this part of his family lore, Bob indicated that when his kids were younger, he would often go outside of the house at night. When the kids were almost asleep he would softly whisper . . .

"Robin, Bobby, Dawn . . . This is Wanda . . . Good night my Darlings."

According to Bob, upon hearing this, his kids would jump out of bed and run into the living room yelling: "It's Wanda! It's Wanda! Did you hear her?"

Bob finished his story about Wanda by stating that whenever he wanted to get the kids out of his hair, he would comment that they should go look for "Wanda's Magical Cave." Armed with that suggestion, his kids would take off to Point Dune in search of their "special friend's Magical Cave."

———

At this juncture in the narrative about Jim's life, you're probably asking yourself something like: "That's a lovely fairy tale, but what in heaven's name does it have to do with Jim's life?"

Well, I'm about to tell you.

———

According to Bob, in fact Wanda the Mermaid was a frequent visitor to their relationship. She may have even made occasional appearances on the ski slopes, immediately after Jim crashed and burned, and at other (in)appropriate moments in their times together.

However, Bob has provided me with two body surfing stories that I considered the most apt when writing about Jim's life.

———

The first story involved something near and dear to both Bob and Jim's heart: The annual Oceanside World Body Surfing Championship competitions.

As related by Bob, Wanda made frequent appearances at their annual fierce competitions at the pier venue.

The context within which she surfaced was usually along the following lines.

———

Wanda's role in their relationship began many years ago. Bob and Jim annually battled each other in the world body surfing championships. Because they were in the same division, they would always try to out-position each other to gain the advantage on the next set of rideable waves.

According to Bob's recollection, he often won the competitions because he was able to position himself to get the better waves. Over and over again, Jim would just miss out on the best waves of the heat, and somehow Bob would catch them.

At the end of the contest Jim would complain bitterly to Bob that Bob was just flat lucky when it came to catching waves. Year after year, Jim insisted that if he had access to equally good waves, he would have whooped up on Bob.

Bob's response to that claim was always the same. He would inform his BFF Jim that he was guided in his wave selection by Wanda, the Magical Mermaid. He would go on and once again advise Jim that because Jim was such a skeptic about Wanda's existence, she would never help him.

Of course Jim's response was just to laugh and grumble at all this BS that he was receiving from his buddy, Bob.

As related by Bob, the Wanda story got to be an ongoing joke between them. When things weren't going Jim's way, regardless of the situation, Bob would always offer the same observation. He would say to Jim, whether the context was surfing, relations with the ladies, skiing, or whatever . . . "Jim, the problem is that you do not believe in Wanda!"

Jim would just guffaw and shake his head in disbelief.

———————

Now the second Wanda story provided by Bob.

One time Wanda illegally crossed the border into Mexico without permission of the Mexican immigration authorities.

The occasion involved Jim and Bob being in Puerto Escondido, Mexico, surfing the famous Mexican pipeline, called Zicatela.

Bob was taking photos of Jim surfing down the line, right at him. As Bob recalls, Jim had just gotten a beautiful 8-foot wave and Bob was taking wonderful pictures of the sports spectacular coming towards him. Unfortunately, at the last moment, Jim had an epic wipeout and the wonderful wave absolutely crushed him.

Jim came up spluttering directly in front of Bob. He immediately began cursing: "Damn it, I lost my new dive watch!!"

Bob reported that Jim was truly upset. However, Bob said to him: "Let's wait for a lull in the set [in Bob's words, "the water was gin clear"]. Maybe we can see it on the bottom with the help of WANDA!"

That suggestion went over with Jim like a lead balloon. He was absolutely infuriated and he swam away in complete disgust to the outside break.

In the meantime, as related by Bob:

> "Stubborn as I am, I waited, and started looking on the bottom. Then I spotted an object just ahead of me. I

ducked down . . . Grabbed it . . . AND IT WAS HIS WATCH!"

Not one to miss such an incredible opportunity to give a ginormous yank to his good buddy's chain, Bob said to himself: "Ah!!! . . . time to really put it to him."

So Bob swam out to where Jim was located in the outside break surf line. When he reached Jim, he swam up close and said:

"Bruin, your problem is you do not believe in Wanda!"

Bob told me that for a moment he thought that Jim was going to punch him. Instead, Jim's immediate response was to curse at him in a very angry tone: "F**k that Wanda Sh*t, Bob!!" *[Editor's note: After all, this narrative is PG rated.]*

Bob's response was a big belly laugh. He then opened his hand and, to Jim's total amazement, showed Jim his watch.

On this occasion, Jim may have laughed even harder than Bob. After he recovered from his convulsive laughter, Jim looked over at his buddy Bob, and said: "Okay Bob, I'm finally a Wanda believer."

Bob finished the story by stating to me that Wanda was a significant part of their brotherly love for so many years and many laughs together. To Bob, Wanda the Mermaid was very much a part of his extraordinary memories of Jim Enright.

———————

On a personal note, I've been in the North County since 1971. I think I can remember when they first started the "world championships" at the Oceanside pier. At its inception, the event had a lot of room for growth.

Now it is truly the World Body Surfing Championships. Competitors come from all over the world. It's a mega event, thanks to the foresight and organizational efforts of our good friend Jim.

Jim's passion for the ocean didn't escape the notice of the local community. In Jim's Memorial materials, they noted that fact in a 1981 front-page sports section article in the old *Blade Tribune* newspaper.

The article was entitled "Jim Enright's 30 Year Love Affair with the Ocean." The article featured a couple of large photos of Jim body surfing.

The newspaper article quoted Jim about his passion for the sport and the ocean. Quotes like: "It takes a nice wave to complete the day," and body surfing as a "way of life, that's what it is to me. I couldn't conceive of being anyplace else."

[And the Tuesday Morning Gang chorus emits a loud "AMEN!!"]

In the article, according to Jim, body surfing or riding a longboard were the keys to his vitality. In addition, his passion for the ocean afforded him a 1,500 to 2,000 yard daily swimming workout for years.

Jim related in the article that the ocean "listened to his problems, exercised him and soothed his days." Jim went on to state: "It's a thrill to get into the perfect wave . . . the perfect shoulder, an extended ride . . . It always feels good."

[And the TMG chorus shouts out another round of "AAAMENS!!!"]

Jim's passion for the ocean was carried over to the battles against beach erosion and beach overbuilding. To again quote the newspaper article, Jim indicated that he was absolutely tuned into the ocean and aware of its significance at both the personal and global levels.

Hey campers . . . listen up. This is an astrophysicist talking here!

———————

Back to Jim's all-around athletic skills.

In addition to his incredible accomplishments as a Waterman and bicyclist, Jim was a bodacious black diamond snow skier on Mammoth Mountain, Sun Valley, and the Ogden, Utah, ski slopes.

And in all of Jim's spare time, he traveled the world, including hiking in the Canadian Rocky Mountains, witnessing spectacular eclipses in Baja California, going to Turkey, Africa, China and Tahiti, as well as traveling in South America. He also visited with relatives in New Zealand and Ireland.

In addition, as Woody Ekstrom is undoubtedly aware, Jim also enjoyed performing with his ukulele group. That was when he wasn't fervently cheering on his UCLA Bruins.

Jim was also known to tip an occasional glass of Tanqueray gin with the Friday Sunset Martini Club.

———————

Gentleman Jim was such a cool dude that I think we need to remember him through two epitaphs/epilogues. The first was delivered in Jim's memorial piece, I believe written by his daughter-in-law.

"Throughout his life, he caught the wave of predicted astronomical discoveries, rode the crest of scientific technological advancement, reflected the *joie de vivre* of his French mother, and, like his Irish father, enjoyed every high-tide-good-time with the thoughtfulness, natural gentility, and a suitable soundtrack."

The second is a wonderful poem written by his surfing buddy, Bob Burnside.

The poem goes as follows:

My Buddy 'Kimo'

Bright days of spring to gift his life
Wonderful years with little strife
Individual and unique. Could he not stay?
Something's missing in our hearts this day
Make like a snowflake, or a falling star.
A wave rushing to shore from afar
A warm soul traveling under an autumn sky
And of him my thoughts. I sigh.
I'll see your smile as the sun goes down
And think of you in the moonlight round
In our Ocean we played
Seeing waves beyond
So once again, on snow slopes will bond
No friend we loved can ever die;
So today I just cannot say "Goodbye"
The outward form but disappears;
My recollection of you is in my tears
Those years our friendship will always remain

There is no way can ever wane
To all I sing that we are bound
You're the best friend, Kimo, I ever found"

And, to close, one more from Bob Burnside:

"My Pal Kimo 'suave con los angelitos' . . . May he always sleep with the little angels."

The
Tuesday
Morning
Gang
Anthology

(Back Row)
Mike Burner, Tommy Dunne, Chuck Lindsay,
Pat O'Connor, Tom Carroll, Tom Keck

(Front Row)
Skip Stratton, Bill Taggart, Woody Ekstrom,
Charley Marvin, Howard Bugbee

(left to right)
Pat O'Connor, Tom Carroll, Chuck Lindsay

(left to right)
Tom Keck, Charley Marvin, Howard Bugbee

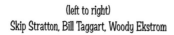

(left to right)
Skip Stratton, Bill Taggart, Woody Ekstrom

(left to right)
Skip Stratton, Howard Bugbee,
Bill Taggart, Charley Marvin

Epilogue

You now have had an opportunity to review some aspects of the amazing lives of the Tuesday Morning Gang.

After reading these heroic tales, I'm sure that any stranger who then attended one of our meetings would end up scratching his head in confusion. His brain would be tied into a pretzel attempting to reconcile these amazing life histories with the reality of the aging and graying citizens gathered on Tuesday mornings around Seaside Market patio tables. Heck, I'm about mid-range age wise in our group, and I'm going to be 79 in July!

How can that guy sitting over there in the wheelchair have once been one of the fastest men in the world?

But it's all true. At least most of it!

And you know what? You know what is the most amazing fact relating to these elderly gentleman?

The answer is their indomitable spirits!!

As an example, you need to look no further than a review of Howard Bugbee's medical history.

Howard, to his credit, has never gotten the memo about the severity of his medical problems. He just ducks his head, dutifully does another rehab, and keeps on motoring with the incredible assistance of his lovely wife Eileen.

Woody Ekstrom has been advised by his doctors that his failing eyesight is going to give out on him fairly soon. Does that slow Woody down? No way with our beloved Woody!

Whatever limited eyesight Woody has left to him will be focused on maintaining his late afternoon and evening rounds at Cap'n Kenos, Vigilucci's, and Papagayo. Not to mention, on occasion, using his extraordinary charm to convince some winsome younger lady to give him a ride home to his beachfront "cottage."

As our stranger looks around the Seaside Market table, he won't be able to believe that some of these old duffers are even still surfing, not to mention skiing!

Thanks for joining me on this journey. I think the trip was worthwhile because, sadly, I believe that God broke the molds when the members of the Tuesday Morning Gang were created.

CPSIA information can be obtained
at www.ICGtesting.com
Printed in the USA
FSHW02n1255220918
52228FS